3 oc

THE LAST SUPPER
ACCORDING TO
MARTHA AND MARY

D1374226

By the Same Author and published by Burns & Oates

REDISCOVERING MARY
Insights from the Gospels

THE LAST SUPPER
ACCORDING TO
MARTHA AND MARY

TINA BEATTIE

crossroad

First published in Great Britain in 2001 by
The Continuum International Publishing Group Ltd
The Tower Building,
11 York Road, London SE1 7NX

First published in the U.S.A. in 2001 by
Crossroad
481 Eighth Avenue, New York
NY 10001 USA

Copyright © Tina Beattie, 2001

All rights reserved. No part of this book may be reproduced, stored
in a retrieval system or transmitted in any form or by any means
whether electronic, mechanical, chemical, photocopying, recording
or otherwise, known or as yet unknown, for any purpose
whatsoever, without the previous written permission of the
publisher.

ISBN 0 86012 290 5 (UK)
ISBN 0 8245 1859 4 (USA)

Typeset by Shelleys The Printers, Sherborne
Printed and bound by Creative Print and Design, Wales

CONTENTS

ANTICIPATION

MARY

Tonight, the stones lament as the sun tips into oblivion. I stand in the small garden behind the house, trying to close the ears of my soul because I'm afraid to listen to the whisper of silence.

The shadow of the olive tree creeps across the ground and fingers my bare feet. I close my eyes, remembering the stroke of my hair on his feet, the touch of his skin on my cheek. Strange man. Strange love. Strange night. Stranger still tonight, this light that fades for the first and last time.

I do not know what it is that I know, nor do I know how I might learn not to know. The breath of the coming night caresses my face. Is there innocence still to be plucked from the gentle air, so that I might suckle its sweetness and taste its oblivion?

I did not want to come to Jerusalem for the passover. I was afraid. I am afraid. He too is afraid. The mood of the crowd has changed, and today when we walked through the city they watched us with sullen faces. How they change, from one moment to the next, as fickle in their hatred as they are in their loving. It is like the storms that billow out of nowhere on the Sea of Galilee, so that men fishing quietly in the starlight suddenly find their boats tossed on the violent waves and their nets ripped by the fury of the sea.

That's how it was that evening, when I went out with the disciples in their boat. We had walked far that day, and everywhere we went the people came to Jesus. Some came to listen and learn, some to argue and debate with him, but many came just to be touched, to be healed, to be blessed by the nearness of his presence.

There were mothers who had brought their children to him in the late afternoon. He was weary by then, and we had been resting together in the shade of a tree. We saw them in the distance, straggling towards us with their babies in their arms and their toddlers by their sides. Peter and Andrew had been into the nearest village to buy food, and they overtook the women. There was a discussion, and then one of the women began shouting and gesticulating at Peter. Jesus seemed irritated. He got up and went over to where they were, and I could see his exhaustion in the way he walked. But he seemed to lighten as he drew close to them. He took one of the babies in his arms and invited the women to come and eat with us. I realized that his irritation was directed at Peter and Andrew, not at the women. He lay in the shadows with the children playing around him and the women gossiping about the small details of their lives.

I was bored and had some sympathy with Peter, for a change. I too would have liked to send them away. My sister Martha was in her element, playing with the children and chatting to the women. They were like sparrows gathered on the branches of a tree, their twitter shattering the silence into a million trifling pieces. Eventually I moved away and sat by myself beside the lake, and there I found peace. I always find peace by myself, a peace that I have only ever been able to share with him.

9

I sat there until the silence muffled their voices, so that I could hear the rustle of the grass and the burr of the crickets and the lapping of the waves on the shore more clearly than I could hear the distant clack of their tongues. I became aware that somebody was watching me. I turned around and found myself staring into the eyes of a small child with a grimy face and tousled hair.

I do not enjoy the company of children. They have not learned to veil their vision, to disguise their joy and their pain. They make me feel too acutely the challenge of the future and the sorry nonsense of the adult world. This child had a gaze that sucked at the soul and a full and solemn mouth. I had not meant to meet its eyes, but I could not look away. Sometimes, Jesus looks at me like that, with eyes that are windows into mystery, so that I have to hold on to myself in case I am sucked into nothingness or everything. Which? If I knew that, I would know all there is to know.

I could not tell **it to go away, this indeterminate child that might have been boy** or girl. It was part of the landscape, part of the silence. I had in my hand a smooth, round stone that I had been absent-mindedly playing with as I sat there. I extended my hand, and offered the stone to the child. It lifted it between thumb and forefinger and held it up to the light, as if it were a crystal instead of just a dull grey pebble from the shore. It walked slowly down to the water's edge, and I saw that its legs were thin beneath its threadbare tunic. It threw the stone into the lake and watched as the ripples spread out and out, such a grand gesture for one little stone, sinking beneath the surface. The child turned and offered me the wisp of a smile, and then it trailed away through the golden grass to join the women.

I watched as the sun slid slowly towards evening, and burnished clouds went winging upwards across the darkening sky. The lake shimmered and blushed and became a vast mirror of red and gold on the face of the earth. Eventually I realized that the women had gone, and the silence was broken only by a whispering breeze and the call of a dove ruffling the evening air.

Jesus came to sit beside me. I felt his nearness. There was no need for words, although his presence filled my being. He cupped his chin in his hands, gazing out beyond the horizon. The colours of the sunset and the water were reflected on his skin, so that he sat in an aureole of light. I longed to reach out and touch him because I thought perhaps he had become a sunbeam or a mirage reflected from the lake, and his body was simply the light playing tricks on my eyes. So I focused on the muscles knotted in his arms, and the tendons in his neck. I looked at his hands, the hands of a carpenter who has some strange healing in his touch.

I was mesmerised the first time I saw him working, mesmerised by the seductive beauty of his touch. He was making a table for our house in Bethany. The wood lay pale and fragrant beneath his hands, and he used his tools with a gentleness that seemed to mould the wood into shape by sculpting the air around it. He worked with a furrow of concentration on his brow but there was a tranquillity about him. It was the look of a man who was at peace with himself. And yet although he was absorbed in what he was doing, I

11

knew that he was aware of me being there, not as a distraction but as something more subtle and welcoming than that. Inspiration perhaps? As he worked, was he thinking of Martha and me eating at the table with our friends? Did he leave us something of his presence in the grain of the wood and the smooth polished surface so that we might remember him at our mealtimes?

That day by the Sea of Galilee I watched the setting sun and I tried to evoke a sense of a body out of the radiant demi-god who sat beside me, but it was no good. I had to reach out and touch his face, to run my fingers through his beard and rest my hand on his cheek. He caught my hand and pressed it to his lips.

'I can't believe you're real,' I said.

'Look,' he murmured, 'look across the lake.' I looked at the distant blue hills. Pinpricks of firelight signalled the communion of evening. The fires were built by shepherds and fishermen, companions of the night who would remain awake while the stars traced their silver messages across the sky.

His mother once told me that on the night he was born the stars shone with such brightness that the flocks on the hillside became restless, and the shepherds gathered up the lambs and sought shelter in the stable where she had gone to give birth. The birth was difficult and the night was cold. She had been afraid that the baby might die, but one of the shepherds had warmed him as he would have warmed a newborn lamb, cupping him in big gentle hands and holding him in the folds of his cloak until the baby's flesh lost the tinge of death.

Remembering the child with the mournful gaze, imagining the newborn infant in the shepherd's embrace, I felt the tug of something in my soul.

'I'm going to the other side of the lake. Will you come with me?' he said.

'How will you get there?'

'Peter and Andrew will be going fishing soon. I'll go with them.'

I let him pull me to my feet, conscious of the other disciples. They had come to find us and they were standing nearby. I glanced at the women, to see if they were listening. My sister had heard. She caught my eye, and there was a flicker of warning in her gaze. She thought it was inappropriate for me to go across the lake with the men. Perhaps she was afraid too. Since our parents were killed, we have had only each other, and Lazarus, but he is not to be relied upon. He has after all died once already. Who is to say that it will not happen again?

Lazarus offered to be a brother to us. When he wandered into Bethany three years ago, looking for work and a place to live, it seemed sensible to take him in as a brother. We were two women living alone, and the times are not safe. Anyway, Jesus says that we are all his brothers and sisters. We are a family united by spirit and not by blood. Yet if Lazarus were my blood brother, I would not have let him share my bed the way he used to, when our spirits were lonely and our bodies were restless. He would not now look at Martha the way he does, so that I see him dreaming of marriage and children.

13

Martha and I are bound by blood and grief and by bodies that were woven side by side in our mother's womb. I doubt if there is any spirit that could create such a bond of love and loss between two women. What would she do if anything happened to me?

But her fear made me defiant. I looked at the lake, and it was a spirit of water and flame that beckoned to me.

'Yes,' I said, 'Yes, I'll come with you.'

I gathered up my skirts, and I felt Peter's hostility as he helped me into the boat. Peter cannot accept that Jesus calls women as well as men to be his disciples, and he resents me more than all the rest, because Jesus loves me with a special love. He loves Peter too, but Peter will not come close and allow himself to feel the touch of that love on his flesh and the kiss of it on his lips. Peter doesn't dare to receive the extravagance of Jesus' love.

He thinks it is wrong that we women should follow Jesus, forgetting the place assigned to us in the world. He approves of Martha more than me, although Martha too has left her cooking and her chores, and now she follows Jesus with the others. At the end of the day, though, she still delights in being the one who prepares the food and cares for us all. Sometimes I think that I will spend the rest of my life living as I do now, in this space of wild and loving freedom that Jesus offers. But there will come a time when my sister will look up and see the love in Lazarus' eyes, and they will marry and have children, and Jesus will mean something different to her. He will be the source of her motherly love and her tenderness, just as he will always be the source of my passion and my longing.

We set out in Peter and Andrew's boat, and the air was fragrant with the last breath of day. Darkness skimmed the shoreline and smudged the outlines of my sister and the others, watching us from the shore. I trailed my hand in the water and reclined against Jesus, while Peter and Andrew cast their nets and prepared for their evening's work.

The storm came upon us suddenly, with a gusting wind and rain that sliced against our skin. The lake churned and lashed the boat, and it began to dip and tumble amidst the waves. My hair whipped back from my face, and the wind pulled the skin tight against my bones. I looked at Peter and Andrew and saw the terror on their faces, and their fear was kindling to my spirit.

I did not care if we died. I would have been happy to plunge into the blue green heave of the lake with him, to tumble down and down and down to the eternal depths, to feel the last bubble of breath escape from my lungs and surrender myself to his watery love. I turned to see if he too was afraid.

He lay there, leaning back against the prow, and he was asleep like a baby in its mother's arms. The storm and the rocking of the boat, the seething waves, and the wind that whined and snarled in our ears, all these were like a lullaby to him. His face was at peace, and a secret smile played about his lips as if he was having the sweetest of dreams.

'Lord! Lord! The boat is sinking.' Peter's voice was shrill with panic. Jesus awoke and I saw how he fixed his gaze on Peter, as if challenging him. But Peter was in no mood to be challenged. He was trembling, and there was a sob in his voice. 'I have a wife, Lord,' he said, 'and a child. Who will care for them if I die?'

Slowly, Jesus peeled his gaze away from Peter's face and looked out at the sea. Did it happen in an instant or was there just a gradual easing of the storm? I do not know. I only know that there was a time—a moment, an hour?—when time itself stood still, and when the minutes began to pass again the sea was at peace and the wind had dropped to a whisper, and in that whisper I heard words. 'Where is your faith?' 'Where is your faith?' That is what the wind was saying. Or at least, that is what I heard the wind saying. Did Peter hear it too? Where was his faith?

I had faith. Oh, if it is called faith, this passion that would surrender itself even to death, then that night I had all the faith of the prophets and all the faith of history within my breast, but Peter was afraid, and the storm passed, and my faith subsided into some strange sense of regret and a lost opportunity.

So many memories, and why this loss, why this sudden nostalgia as if those times have gone forever? We will sail in Peter's boat again, and I will gaze on the face of Jesus as he sleeps. There will be days and nights ahead when we will love and laugh and cry, surely? I cannot believe that I have discovered this wonder of being, only to lose it. But tonight there is loss all around, and I am afraid with some nameless fear. I was not afraid of the storm, but I am afraid of this silence tonight.

I try to distract myself by remembering a time before Jesus came into our lives, a time when I found meaning in something other than loving him. I think of our house in Bethany, of Martha building with the men day after day, strong arms and capable hands, lifting, hammering, smoothing, working from early morning with the drip of sweat on her brow and her face smeared with grime.

The Romans killed our parents after the last uprising, and a year later they destroyed our home. My mother faced them defiantly, and had I not seen the way her hands tweaked and twitched at her side I would have believed her to be fearless in the face of death. Martha and I huddled in one another's arms, smelling each other's fear. Our father, smaller and more fragile than our mother, stood beside her, rocking backwards and forwards on his heels with his arms folded over his breast. 'Please, please,' he said, over and over again, until the Roman sword cut the breath from his throat. I heard, but I did not see, my mother's death. Did Martha also close her eyes in that final moment? I have never asked her.

After we had anointed and buried their bodies, I thought I would never know peace or joy again. But eventually, after the destruction and the loss, we found a small piece of land in the village, and we began to build a home for ourselves, and slowly, slowly, we felt hope beginning to trickle through our veins. And then the laughter returned.

It was Lazarus who brought laughter back into our lives, and helped us to rediscover our youth. We did not know then that Lazarus was simply the first lightening of the sky before dawn, that soon there would be a sunburst of joy so radiant that sometimes even the stones would seem to laugh with delight in our presence.

So why then tonight do the stones seem to weep?

Small birds flicker against the sky. The evening has soaked up the colours that shimmer on their wingtips. They look like tiny demons, malevolent messengers from a world of pain.

Passers-by straggle home, women's voices rimming the day with chatter, men punctuating their froth with solemn grunts.

Lazarus came when we were beginning to build the house, with his ripe young body ready for work. How beautiful he was, as he worked beside Martha day by day, as he lay beside me in the secret, silent hours of night.

The man I married lacked the energetic beauty of these two I have loved since. I married him soon after the Romans destroyed our home, because Martha and I needed somewhere to live and he said that if I married him, my sister could live with us. He was a small man, and I mistook his weakness for tenderness. At night when I spread my body beneath the gaze of the moon, he turned away. Dutifully he joined himself to me, as if in the furtive begetting of children we might be forgiven for the extravagant delights of the flesh.

But there were no children, and few delights. One day he left, to travel and trade. I kissed him goodbye, and I felt my spirit expand to greet the coming day. I wanted to leave his house with its memories of disappointment, and that's when we began building the house in Bethany. Martha and I started to plan our lives, and in the hidden moments known only to God I begged that my husband might never return.

Lazarus and Martha built the house together, with help from the people in the village. Sometimes I helped, but they said I was too much of a dreamer. Maybe they're right. Sometimes I sang to them, or brought them wine in the heat of the day. Sometimes I danced, weaving the shape of my movements into their work, kneading the air with my body as Martha kneads the dough and the clay with her hands.

The smell of her cooking drifts through the window. She is happy in the kitchen with the other women, preparing the passover meal. She's probably irritated that I'm not in there with them, helping, but the sky and the silence called me away. It's too hot in there, not just the heat of the kitchen but the heat of women, their voices, their companionship that melts and blurs the spaces between them, their round faces and ripe, contented breasts. I am never so lonely as when I am in a roomful of women.

MARTHA

I want the meal to be good tonight. The bread and the lamb cooked to perfection. They will be tired and hungry, and they're all on edge at the moment. It's the tension in the city that's getting through to everybody. I'll make sure they relax—warm water to wash their feet, fine wine, maybe Mary will dance for us after dinner. Jesus loves her dancing as much as he loves my cooking.

Other men love Mary for her body and me for my cooking, but he's different. It's as if he sees some joy and meaning in what we do that even we don't understand. To dance. To prepare a meal for friends. To talk. To sow and harvest crops. To catch fish. Even to collect taxes. All the small activities that fill our lives suddenly seem momentous, shot through with meaning. I am learning at last to be satisfied with the rhythms of my life.

I find myself here in the kitchen handling the food in a new way, with all my senses heightened. The parsley smells clean and crisp and new, flecking my hands with green. There is a sticky sweetness to the dates, so that I can't resist licking my fingers as I work. My hands seem suddenly miraculous in their ordinariness, no longer taunting me with their broad, red practicality but showing me how they delight in what they do. Their deftness with the knife as I slice and chop and stir. Their sensitivity to the ripeness of fruit and the warmth of the dough that rests against my palms. I have never noticed before how many different flavours and smells and sounds there are when a meal is being prepared. The lamb spits and sputters as it bakes, and I am wreathed in its fragrance. The dough has the comforting aura of my mother's skin, when I used to press my face against the softness of her neck. The mustard is pungent and pinches my nostrils. The wine in the jug is a precious jewel that glows red in the candlelight and seduces me with its promise of companionship. How alive I feel, amidst the textures and smells of this womanly world.

And when I listen to myself, I hear things I haven't heard before, as if my words have significance. Mary's words have always had a grace and a charm that capture people's attention and make them sit at her feet to listen. She measures her words out, the only thing in life she knows how to be frugal with. She's reckless in everything else, while I'm the opposite. She used to resent my careful housekeeping, my rationing out of our resources, just as she used to be irritated by my constant foolish chatter.

I used to think she was better than me - clever, beautiful, secret. It's as if when we were in the womb together, she was woven out of the airy cobwebs that knit the stars together, and I was moulded out of the heavy earth.

One day, in a fit of frustration, I said to Jesus that I felt as if my sister was fire and I was clay. He gave me that ironic, lop-sided grin that I cannot quite understand. It makes me feel foolish when he smiles at me like that, although I never feel that he's laughing at me. It's just that he sees things differently. He seems to see the whole picture, while we fret over the details.

'Were not fire and clay made for each other?' he said. We were sitting opposite each other at a table, and there was a jug of wine between us. 'Here,' he said. 'Give me your hands.' Then he cupped my hands in his, and he ran my palms around the contours of the jug. 'Feel how smooth it is, how it asks to be touched,' he said. 'Look. Look at the glaze. See how it holds the colours of the fire.' I looked, and it was true. The jug glowed blue and red and copper, as if the flame that fired it had become part of its essence. 'What use is clay without the flame, Martha?' he said. 'Don't you see? Without clay, the flame would spend its passion in emptiness. Without flame, the clay would have no strength and no shape.'

He is teaching me to love my sister without envy, and it is as if a burden that I have carried around all my life is gradually lightening.

Jesus loves Mary. He too is a spirit of cobweb and starlight, and I think his soul finds some answering echo in her that he finds nowhere else. They rarely speak, but they sit together long after everyone else is in bed, and their silence breathes some strange presence through the house, so that when I get up in the morning, I can still feel it lingering.

But Jesus loves me too. He's also a creature of the earth, a hungry, gregarious man who eats and drinks and laughs and sometimes talks too much, and says the wrong thing in the wrong place so that everyone takes offence. If Mary is his companion in silence and the solitude of night, then I am his companion in laughter and the conversations of daily life, and for the first time ever I realize that my role is as important as hers.

In the past, men who have known Mary and me have always made us feel competitive, as if we could only be valued one at a time. Those who love her wildness treat me like a mother, happy for me to be in the kitchen while she entertains them. Those who prefer my company find Mary terrifying, a woman who won't be tamed.

I used to think she gave nothing, my sister. I felt consumed by her, drained and exhausted by the effort of living so close to such nameless and restless desire. 'What do you want?' I used to say, and she would cry out, 'I don't know. I don't know.' So I would give more, trying to be mother and father and sister and friend, giving all that I knew how to give, thinking I received nothing in return.

But now I realize that Mary also gives. She gives of her spirit and her breath. Her body is sharp, her voice breathes passion and fury. And yet she loves, how Mary loves. I've seen Mary love before, but not like this. She burns with a fire that sets her aglow—not consuming but replenishing her, as if she has discovered the source of the life that fires the universe. Sometimes I marvel at how quickly our lives have changed, and I wonder how we came to discover this strange intensity, this peculiar joy and terror that has become our way of being.

For so many years, our lives hardly changed at all. Time was a wide river that carried us serenely through gentle landscapes, and the years sat sunning themselves on the banks and watched us go by. We measured our progress in the creeping changes that imperceptibly left their mark upon us as we slept. Our mother's black hair grew silver threads, and cobwebs of laughter spun themselves around her eyes and mouth. Our father went bald, so that I loved to run my palm over the shiny dome of his head. I saw my sister lose the shapeless freedom of her childhood, and in her awkward new body I glimpsed the dark beauty of a woman struggling to be born. I felt my own body softening and curving, becoming like my mother's, and in my dreams I heard the laughter of children from further along the river.

Then I awoke, not to laughter but to whirlpools and rapids and the terror of drowning. The slice of a soldier's sword ended forever that tranquil journey through time. My mother's hair never would turn silver, and the traces of laughter around her eyes would remain forever sketched on my memory as the thwarted promise of her old age. My father's poor head lay puddled in blood, never again to feel the laughing caress of a daughter's hand.

Once I thought that perhaps Lazarus and Mary and I would recreate the contentment of our youth, but instead Jesus has taught us to swim in the whirlpools and survive in the rapids. I have stopped longing for the wide lazy days and the gentle passing of time. Now I wait for these moments of calm at the end of the day, and I make them last forever. I have discovered how to create a feast out of nothing, a paradise out of ordinariness, a lifetime of joy out of an evening of friendship. I did not know before how little one needs to have everything worth having.

DOUBT

MARTHA

Mary of Magdala arrives, breathless and pale.

'There's been a fight in the street outside,' she says. Her fear ripples through us.

'Who?'

'Judas and one of the other Zealots, a man called Benjamin.'

'What was it about?' I ask, although I know. We all do.

'A bunch of Zealots were waiting for us near the temple. They began following us, taunting Judas. This man Benjamin seemed to be their spokesman. He said Judas has betrayed them, that Jesus is a pawn in the hands of the Romans. He's taking away our fighting spirit and making us weak and passive.'

'What did Judas do?'

'You know what he's like. He lost his temper and hit the man. They got into a fight. Some of the other disciples separated them, and the Zealots went off into the night, looking for trouble no doubt.'

'And Judas?'

'For a moment it looked as if he might go with them, but he stayed with us. I think he feels humiliated, as if he can't make up his mind what he's fighting for any more.'

'Did Jesus see what was happening?'

'No, he arrived afterwards, when it was all over. He'd been delayed further back, on his way through the city. He was upset about something. Somebody said he was weeping.'

Oh, I can't bear this. The blood and the tears and the fury and the grief. That's the other side of this story, the one I choose not to think about. I want to hold onto the friendship and love, the delight of his company. But he brings trouble too. Wherever he goes, there's trouble. Who does he think he is?

Sometimes, I think it's not worth all this. I can see the scene in the street, vivid and alive in my imagination. I can see it because it's happened before— the brawls, the violence, the aggression he unleashes in men. No wonder he prefers the company of women.

Benjamin the Zealot, with revolution in his gaze and murder in his voice, tormenting Judas.

'Ha! Here he comes, poor lamb. Changing the world, are you Judas? Liberating your people? Be nice to everyone. Love your enemies. Turn the other cheek. How touching! We're all so happy for you, Judas, aren't we, men?' He would turn round to enjoy the shouts and curses of his friends. 'Why, if you were a bit nicer to look at, we might even fall in love with you ourselves, now that you've become a woman. Pity about the beard though, Judas. You ought to think of shaving.' They would degenerate into coarse abuse then, and Judas would glower and fume until his anger erupted. It's happened before. It will happen again.

Sometimes I feel sorry for Judas. He is a man of conviction and courage. He dares to stand up for what he believes, to fight for what's right. I can remember when I first met him. He was speaking to a crowd gathered outside the city walls, and I was on my way into the city from Bethany. I stopped to listen. My

27

father was a Zealot. That's why they killed him. I don't know why they had to kill my mother as well, but they did. Ever since, I've been repelled and seduced by the message the Zealots preach.

Judas' voice rolled across the open spaces, and the people were captivated.

'We wait like lambs for the eagle to swoop,' he said. 'The Romans make a mockery of us. They reduce us to servitude and humiliate our people. But we will fight for our freedom and our dignity. Like Moses, we will lead our people out of bondage. Even if our exodus takes us through the wilderness of hunger and death, we will persevere until we reach the promised land of liberation for the poor, liberation for the orphan and the widow, liberation for God's people who have suffered too long and too silently at the hands of our oppressors. We will bring about the day of the Lord's favour, when the captives will be set free and the blind will see. We are a people destined for greatness, and we will fulfil our destiny.'

I used to wonder why Judas followed Jesus. Then one day I realized: it's because he recognized a kindred spirit. They share the same vision, they hold out the same promises, they appeal to the same people. They are men with voices that captivate and dreams that mesmerise. They both want to change the world. Judas would do it with the sword. And Jesus? How will he bring about the liberation he dreams of? With words of love and a healing touch? Sometimes I think we are mad to follow him. What can words do against the empire of Rome?

But when he speaks of love and forgiveness, when he urges us to turn away from violence and vengeance, when I watch him touching and healing and feeding the people, I catch sight of some new and undreamed-of possibility, as if the whole human race might be on the brink of discovering its real nature and its true way of being.

Then I think of the Romans and their brutality, I think of my parents, my mother's blood spurting from her throat as her dying breath gurgled in her lungs, and I have moments of terrible doubt. What if the Zealots are right? What if we're being deceived? Our young men are willing to resist, to fight to the death if necessary. They feel abandoned by Judas. And what will we do, if the Romans begin another slaughter of our people? They crucified five men today—thieves and murderers they say. Who are they to judge, with their armies and their laws and their taxes?

Jesus says we should pay our taxes, but I'm not so sure. When he speaks like that, I glance at Judas and I see the furrows deepen around his mouth. And yet, even in those moments, there's a strange similarity between them. Sometimes, in the half-light of evening before the lamps are lit, I can hardly tell them apart.

Isn't it true that those who are most alike experience their differences most acutely? Mary and I, twins in our mother's womb, mirrors to one another's faces and moods and expressions, and yet magnifying our differences, desperate to mark the spaces between us, to define ourselves, to know who we are by knowing who we are not. Such is the relationship I glimpse between Jesus and Judas. Twins of the spirit, in the same way that Mary and I are twins of the flesh.

Sometimes I think that if Jesus fails we will all turn to Judas and we might hardly be able to tell the difference. All of us except Mary.

Mary despises Judas now, although it hasn't always been that way. Last week, she accused him of stealing the money we collect for the poor. She burst into the room singeing the air with her fury, hair wild about her face, pale eyes like the blue that glows at the hottest part of the flame, where her gaze meets the kindling of her soul. I watched the heave of her breast in her low-bodiced dress, the thrust of her hand towards him, the wanton tilt of her body.

Mary's body speaks a language all of its own. Men think they understand that language, but they don't. The desire that flares around her is not for any human form. It's a nameless hunger that makes my sister's spirit prowl the night, that erupts from her in the wildness of laughter and tears and gestures that shatter the bounds of her physical presence.

They don't understand. That's why they dragged her, naked and proud, from Lazarus' bed.

I felt sorry for Judas. There she stood, hand on hip, other hand thrust towards him.

'The money, Judas. I want the money we collected today. There's a woman in the kitchen with her daughter. They're hungry. They have nowhere to sleep. I want to give them money to pay for food and a bed.' I knew that Mary was just being provocative. She is usually the last to respond, the last to attend to the poor. It's not that she's heartless, but she rarely notices the needs of those around her. She seems to live in a kind of impenetrable solitude. But that night she had found something with which to goad Judas, and it was too good an opportunity to miss.

'Where are they from, this woman and her child?' he asked. She narrowed her eyes, thrust her jaw forward, ready for a fight.

'Samaria.'

'Why should we give money to Samaritans? Aren't there enough hungry Jews?'

'Hunger doesn't ask where a person comes from, and neither do we. That's the rule, remember Judas? All the poor, all the needy.'

'And what happens to all this money we give away? We give the poor money for food, and tomorrow we give them more money for food, and on and on it goes.' He stepped towards her, and his anger was coiled like a spring in his body. I thought he might hit her. 'We are numbing them to their poverty, keeping their suffering at bay to make them complacent. There are other ways of using money to help the poor, Mary. That money can buy swords, it can feed strong young men and build a fighting force to overthrow the Romans. Then we can set our people free. Then there will be no beggars, no hungry women and children.'

I watched them, facing each other across a small space. The rest of us were silent, as we always are when Mary and Judas confront each other. I don't know how it would have ended if Jesus hadn't arrived at that moment. Usually he defends Mary, but for a moment it seemed as if he might take Judas' side.

'Why should we help a Samaritan woman, Mary?' he asked. 'Judas is right. There are enough of our own kind who stand in need of help.' He was goading her now, just as she had goaded Judas. A weaker woman might have felt trapped and defeated by these two men, but my sister does not give in so easily. She turned to Jesus and her body spoke differently, rearranged itself, melted into warm desire. No wonder people gossip about those two.

'She is my kind. She's a woman. She has a daughter. I'm a woman, a daughter. You would not turn them away.'

'What if I did?' She narrowed her eyes and for a moment her body was sharp and angry again.

'If you did, you wouldn't be the person I believe you to be.'

He laughed then, that great gusty laugh that always surprises me because it seems to create hurricanes of joy in the room.

'Judas, the money we collect is for bread, not swords. Give me the money. Mary, call the woman and her daughter. Invite them to eat with us.'

Oh, I get so exasperated when he does that. As if I can work miracles with the food we have.

'What if there's not enough food?' I said, and I noticed that Judas smiled at me like an ally. Jesus laughed again, in high spirits.

'Martha, Martha,' he said. 'There's always enough food.' Which was true enough. But even so, there's always a first time. . . .

And yet how I love these meals when he brings his friends and calls strangers off the street and we sit together late into the night. When he is among us conversation flows like wine into the cups and hollows of the night that nestle between the satisfied bodies of people who have eaten and drunk well.

I put my arm round Mary of Magdala, and I feel her trembling. She leans her head on my shoulder.

'He's in danger,' she whispers.

'Who? Judas?'

'Both of them. Judas and Jesus. They both have enemies. Sometimes I think they've become enemies to one another. The way Judas looks at him. The way he looked tonight. Broken. Bitter. He used to be so passionate, so full of conviction and spirit. I'm not sure, I'm not sure he should have followed Jesus. He needs to fight. It's not for him, all this tramping round the countryside telling stories and healing people.'

'Mary, Mary,' I say, rocking backwards and forwards and stroking her hair. 'You forget yourself. Where would you be, if it weren't for the healing?' I feel Mary shivering, as she remembers the demons of madness that possessed her and sent her into frenzies of despair.

Ruth is watching us, Ruth who was trapped in a broken and twisted body for eighteen years, until that sabbath day when she encountered Jesus at the temple. We had all known Ruth and had pitied her from a distance. Sometimes I took her food, and in winter I tried to make sure that she had a cloak to wrap around herself as she begged outside the temple gates. And then that day, he touched her lightly as he passed and he said something to her, and Ruth's body was like the fragile wings of a butterfly as it emerges from its cocoon, spreading and growing and blossoming in the sunlight.

Ruth is pregnant. After he healed her, she became a disciple. She and Andrew fell in love, and now she is pregnant with his child. Those of us who knew her during the barren years of her illness are delighted, but people gossip about her. They gossip about all the women disciples. They say it's wrong for us to mix so freely with men, to wander about the countryside the way we do. Ruth's pregnancy confirms their suspicions. They think we're all harlots. They have never forgotten Mary's humiliation, when Jesus saved her from stoning. I still can't bear to think of that day, of my sister's nakedness and the leering men who surrounded her. Most of them were jealous. They envied Lazarus. They had lusted after her for years.

Maybe in their eyes she is a harlot—a married woman who shared her bed with another man. Naomi and Rachel worked in a brothel before they became disciples. People say they continue their work even now among the male disciples. Once we would have been upset by such rumours, but Jesus has taught us to laugh instead. 'Take the plank out of your own eye,' he tells the gossips, 'before you try to remove the speck of dust in somebody else's eye.'

The crowds don't know what to make of his humour. I'll never forget the day our leaders gathered around to question him, and he sat drinking wine with us and laughing, making light of their questions, as they became more and more agitated. That's when he told them they had swallowed a camel and strained out a gnat. How we laughed! But there is danger in talking like that, and we all know it. Sooner or later, they will have their revenge.

I rock backwards and forwards with Mary Magdala in my arms, and Ruth watches us with her round belly and her anxious face. There are flurries of fear in the room. I look at the women's faces. Joanna, Rachel, Mary Salome. Then I look at his mother. She arrived with Mary Magdala, and she is still wearing her cloak. She is framed in the window in the last light of day, so that I see only her silhouette. She looks vast and impenetrable against the light. Is she afraid? What is she thinking?

'Mary?' I say. She doesn't answer. Slowly, she lifts her arms, and her blue cloak seems to form a canopy against the darkness. I am drawn to her, and the others follow me. We huddle there, enfolded in her arms. I bury my face against her shoulder and feel the rise and fall of her breathing. We are still, so still that I begin to feel her heart beating against my breast. Ruth's belly is pressed against my back, and I feel the squirm of her baby in the womb.

Now we are all in some primal womb, before any word is spoken, before the spirit moves on the face of the void, bodies no longer but earth and the promise of life that swirls in the breath of God. Seeds buried deep in the soil, silent and lifeless, non-being, non-woman, not dead but waiting to be born, waiting to become women who know what it is to give birth, the blood and the water and the tearing apart of our tender flesh and the emptying out of the fruits of our love.

She pushes us gently away. We separate, each restored to her own body and her own name, but tranquil now, as if his mother has absorbed our anxiety and our fear. Now more than ever I am determined that this will be a night to remember.

'Come,' I say, 'we must prepare the meal. They'll be here soon.' And I speak with the voice of Martha, busy, domesticated, motherly Martha, when only a moment ago I melted with these women and became the breath of God.

MARY

A pale moon rises over the rooftops. Houses snuggle together beneath the darkness, spilling yellow lamplight from their windows. People are gathering for the passover. Laughter trickles through doorways and somewhere I hear the high, lonely cry of a child. I look up to the kitchen window, hearing the chatter of Martha and the other women. As I watch, Mary his mother comes to stand in the window. She looks down and sees me in the garden. Our eyes meet, and I know that she also knows. I want her to come down to me, to tell me what it is that we know. Perhaps she can give a shape and a name to this sense of foreboding. But she turns away, and as I watch, she raises her arms and blocks out the light, and I am alone again.

I begin to wander through the streets of the city. A cat slinks across my path and stands watching with mean eyes. Jerusalem broods tonight, like a beast that stirs and hunts in darkness. They say there will be trouble. I listen to the slap of my sandals on the paving stones, the gasp and fret of the city, the ocean of silence that slurps and sucks at the edges of night and guzzles the life of the world. A man lurches at me from the shadows, and I smell death on his breath. He staggers and mumbles obscenely, and I feel the clutch of his hand on my arm. I shake him off, but I try to be gentle. He is too old and drunk to threaten me, and I sense the newborn soul that whimpers in his gaze and begs for love, dimly remembering the taste of a mother's breast.

I thread my way through the city streets, as if a magnet draws me to the temple walls. Jesus spoke this week of destroying the temple, and I felt the heaving fury of the people, the same people who had waved palm branches and welcomed him into the city. Now with this presentiment growing stronger within me, I must go and touch the walls and remind myself how strong they are.

Sometimes he speaks in strange images, with words that veil the truth of what he says. So it was with the temple, surely. 'Destroy this temple and I will build it again in three days.'

The hairs on my arms prickled at his audacity. He stood there with the walls looming behind him, his arms raised towards them in an absurd gesture that only emphasized how small he was, a man among men, unremarkable, ordinary, without any special beauty or majesty, nothing really to look at. But the crowds heaved around him when they heard what he was saying, and they growled and rumbled like an earthquake gathering beneath us, so that for a moment I thought that they were indeed capable of destroying the temple.

And what of the man who faced them? Was he really capable of rebuilding it? I wanted to take him in my arms then, to lure him away to our house in Bethany, to protect him from the madness of his dreams. And yet another part of me wanted to share his dreams, to cry out to the crowd and make them listen. But they could not listen, because they made so much noise. To hear what he says, it's not enough to pay heed to his words. It is his silence that really speaks. And who in these times is willing to listen to silence? Even I, tonight, would rather have words than the spaces between them.

I come to the end of the narrow street and the darkening sky tumbles about my ears. Across the way the temple rests like a mother in the midst of her brood, pale and serene in the moonlight. I make my way to the west wall, and there I stand in silence and listen to the stones lamenting.

It's louder here, this inaudible sob which shifts and stirs the currents of night. I stand with my palms on the rocks, and they live and breathe beneath my touch. They breathe with the rhythms of his body when late at night I rest my ear against his breast and listen to the beating of his heart. The temple too has a heart that beats, a heart that beats for the people he loves. I rest my ear against the cold rock, and I hear the heart of the world breaking.

THIRST

MARTHA

They arrive, hot and dusty and agitated, the twelve men and five women who stayed with them while we came to prepare the meal—Rebecca, Elizabeth, Rachel, Hannah, and Sarah. Rachel's children are with them, chattering and babbling. The children are tired and hungry but innocent of the menace in the air. Their voices burble on the edges of the adults' conversation. The adults laugh and joke, but they can't disguise the tension that chokes the laughter in their throats.

Rachel's voice and her laughter are louder than the rest, as if she still has to assert her presence among us, to declare herself in the face of the men's scepticism. She stands among us with Samuel on her hip and Sharon hanging on her skirts, with her red hair glinting in the lamplight and her eyes sparking mischief at the men. Rachel delights me with her effrontery. My sister Mary glowers with a dark sensuality that comes from somewhere deep within her, but Rachel wears her sexuality like a new dress, flouncing and flirting and mocking the men with her good-humoured beauty.

She comes to stand beside me and offers Samuel a crust of bread from the table where I am working. I envy Rachel her children. Samuel's arm rests plumply against her breast, and his small fist curls around her cheek.

'Hey my precious one,' she laughs, jiggling the child on her hip. 'You're not going to sleep, are you? We're just about to have a party. Look at the feast that Martha is preparing.' The child watches me from beneath lowered lashes, too sleepy to respond. Sharon twines her arms around my legs, jealous of the attention being paid to her brother.

'What are you cooking, Martha?' she asks. I bend down and lift her in my arms. At three she is still small enough to fit snugly against me, and suddenly I crave the child's reassuring nearness. At times when our adult world seems precariously close to the edge of dread, children anchor us in the land of the living. Sharon's flushed cheeks and bright eyes, her body fidgetting against mine, seem like the small gestures of a world that refuses to surrender its hold on the blessed ordinariness of life.

I show her the lamb with its crisp golden layer of fat.

'Breathe in,' I say. 'Close your eyes and smell how good it is.' She closes her eyes and breathes deeply. I laugh, and so does she. She clasps my face between her hands and kisses me. I laugh again. I dip my finger in the wine and put it in her mouth to suck. The sucking calms her. She droops against my shoulder and I feel the tug of her tongue like a little animal burrowing against my finger. How I long for a child.

I find myself looking for Lazarus, and then I discover that his eyes have already found me, and they respond to my gaze. I blush. What is this? I smile at him over Sharon's head, and he returns my smile. The smile of a man who has returned from the grave is without parallel in this world. It knows of a suffering and a peace beyond anything we can imagine. Lazarus has been to no-time, no-place, no-words, no-thing. Lazarus has been dead. And now his smile holds out some strange promise of life to me across the room and from the other side of the tomb, and I press Sharon's body to myself and feel the beginning of wonder within me, like the first stirrings of a child in the womb.

I turn and see Rachel watching me. I give her a rueful smile. She raises an eyebrow, and a bubble of laughter escapes from her. She nudges me, and spontaneously we hug one another, needing to share something beyond words. I smell the musk of her armpits from a day's walking, and I feel her energy reinvigorating me. There's a vitality to Rachel, which isn't sapped by exhaustion and fear. Perhaps it comes from having to stay alive in the face of so much abuse and disappointment. I marvel at her optimism and her good humour.

She loves to recount how she met Jesus at the well, how he spoke to her even though she kept her eyes averted and tried to look modest. She was angry at first, tired of being used by men, tired of the fact that they only ever saw her as a body that might gratify their needs. She tried to fend him off, but she was fascinated in spite of herself. He too was needy, like the other men she met. He said he was thirsty, but she sensed he was asking her for much more than a drink of water. What did he want?

As she bantered and flirted, she came to realize that whatever he was asking for, it wasn't her body. He spoke about giving her so much water that she would never have to go to the well again. She wanted to kiss him and hug him and thank him, because she was so weary of that daily journey to the well. She had too many children and too little energy, and she no sooner arrived home with her jug of water than they seemed to drain it empty, and she was left with the prospect of a night of thirst, or another journey to the well.

For a moment, she believed she would do anything at all for the water he promised. But then he told her to fetch her husband, and she decided it was a trap. 'I have no husband,' she told him, baiting him. 'Yes, you're right. You've had five, and the one you're with now isn't your husband,' he responded, holding her defiant stare, meeting her challenge.

She was astonished. She thought nobody knew about her new man. Her fifth husband had left, declaring himself fed up with her noisy children and her sluttish ways. She had decided never to get involved with a man again, but the children needed food and clothes, and she had no money, and this new man was a wealthy merchant whose wife wanted silk and furs but not the children of his passion. So he came to her at night, and he paid her well. He was a kind enough lover, and she fed her children and even had enough left to buy some clothes for herself. Now she clutches Samuel against her breast and gives a loving welcome to the fruit of another brief love. Some might say he's just another hungry child, another source of poverty and struggle, but Rachel never seems to see it that way. Her children flow out of some chaotic excess of loving, an inconvenience perhaps, but part of life's lavish and unruly abundance.

But this stranger at the well seemed to know her story, and she wondered how he knew. She felt his gaze on her, seeing her, all of her. Men had looked at her before, stripping her, staring through her clothes, but this was different. His gaze did not lust or seek to possess. It was a caress, to be sure, but not a caress that was a prelude to seduction. His gaze told her that he loved her, which was ridiculous, since he had only just met her. His gaze told her that he knew her, but how was that possible? She was known and loved. Rachel. Not Rachel the harlot, Rachel the mother, Rachel the wife. Just Rachel. Beautiful in his eyes. Innocent in his eyes. Redeemed? Ah yes, surely redeemed, if redemption meant seeing your own being come to perfection in the presence of another's love.

The male disciples were outraged, although they didn't dare show it. They never have understood why Jesus seeks out the company of women, and although they can tolerate it when he mixes with respectable Jewish women, they thought it a scandal that he should be found alone with a Samaritan woman. They muttered among themselves, and still some of them mock her when Jesus isn't around. But Rachel has coped with worse than that, and she laughs too loudly and speaks with a brash confidence so that they never see the pain in her eyes, the lonely waiting for Jesus to return, and to look at her, and to remind her that she, Rachel, is precious in his eyes, whatever the rest might say.

Jesus comes into the kitchen to greet us, and Elizabeth follows close behind. She is old now, Elizabeth, and there is a heaviness that has never left her since the death of her son. I wonder sometimes what God is about. Why give a woman a child in her old age, a blessed child who proclaims the coming of the Messiah and declares himself a prophet, if he is going to be the cause of her desolation? They beheaded him, Elizabeth's eccentric son who wandered the wilderness and captivated us all with his message.

Elizabeth goes to Mary the mother of Jesus and they hold each other in a long embrace. There's an intuitive bond between these two women that goes far beyond the intimacies of ordinary friendships. Sometimes at night, when we are all sitting together, they entertain us with their reminiscences. I try to remember the stories they tell, because I think that one day these stories will matter to people. They will want to hear about Elizabeth's barrenness, about Mary's strange pregnancy, about the passion and conviction that fired these women and made them the companions of God.

Elizabeth has white hair that wisps like a halo about her head and skin that is the texture of crumpled silk. Mary bears a startling resemblance to her son, with the same sleek dark hair now streaked with silver like my mother's, strong bones that sometimes make her face look as if it is sculpted in stone, but eyes so soft that their gaze strokes the soul like a lover's caress, and a wide mouth that gives shape to the laughter and the grief of her heart.

I have watched these two women with the twinkle of conspiracy between them, giggling like young girls about the circumstances of their pregnancies until tears of mirth run down their faces. Mary mimics the gossips in Nazareth, the old women eyeing her up and wondering whose child it was, the men with their patronizing sympathy for Joseph. Elizabeth shakes her head and parodies her husband's dumb astonishment, when he refused to believe she was pregnant and lost the power of speech until the baby was born. They clutch each other and rock backwards and forwards and shriek with laughter, leaving the rest of us feeling too sober for comfort.

Sometimes they sing Mary's hymn of exultation, 'He has cast the mighty from their thrones, and exalted the lowly, the poor he has filled with good things, the rich sent empty away.' Then their eyes burn and they become creatures of some wondrous realm where all things are possible, and the rest of us sit swaddled in our ordinariness and marvel at the world they describe. Is it really true, that God has cast down the mighty and fed the hungry? Sometimes I want to shout at Mary for being so outrageous. Her child was born in a stinking stable. Her friends' children were murdered by Herod while she fled in terror to Egypt. She refuses to accept that she might have been wrong. She insists that she knows, she knows that none of that is true, not true in the sense of being the ultimate and final truth about the world. One day, she says, one day, God will prove me right. Mary's self-assurance leaves me speechless with admiration and sometimes, when I'm tired and discouraged, with exasperation. I have never known a woman with such confidence. My sister's confidence is a mask for her vulnerability, but Mary seems convinced in the depths of her being that she cannot be wrong. In anybody else it would be insufferable vanity. In Mary, somehow, it becomes the shape of God's promise that gives us strength to follow her wild and crazy son.

But if Mary never loses her confidence, sometimes she loses her radiance. Sometimes, she sits in Elizabeth's arms and they gaze into some distant, hidden world. What do they see there? Do they see the weapons and wealth of the mighty, the faces of children who starve on the streets? Do they pray in their hearts: 'How long, God, how long until Mary's vision is fulfilled?' I have heard these women laugh and sing, but I have also seen them weep and clutch each other with a sorrow that reaches to the bowels of the earth. They are women chosen by God. How glad I am not to be chosen.

Elizabeth's son baptised my sister Mary, soon after we finished building our house in Bethany. She went down into the Jordan in her white shift, a solitary figure, moving with slow determination as if she had some clear purpose in mind. I remember the way she faced him, standing up to her waist in the river, chin tilted, waiting for him to refuse.

That was when Lazarus had just arrived in Bethany, and people were beginning to gossip. John preached the repentance of sin. Mary said there was no sin in her love for Lazarus, but the people of the village didn't agree. There were no complaints when she shared her bed night after night with a husband who repelled her, but when she gave herself freely to the man she loved they were quick to condemn her. People would rather we lied with our flesh than lay bare the restless spirit that calls us into a truthful world of risk and pain. I do not know what it is to experience that restless call of the spirit, but my sister does.

That's why she looked at John in that way. She was challenging him to define what he meant by sin. Would he bless her honest, loving body in the waters of baptism, or would he confer his blessing only on the worthy men and women who masked their loneliness beneath the complacent lies of the flesh?

But of course, the Baptist too was honest in his love and no respecter of convention. I saw the smile of recognition in his eyes, the exchange of glances that sealed their friendship as surely as if they had cut their veins and mingled their blood. I heard the words of her baptism ring out across the valley, and I saw her shameless, voluptuous immersion in the waters.

She came up glistening, a newborn virgin emerging from the womb of the earth, untouched and untouchable. She waded out of the river and climbed the bank towards me, and I was glad there were no men around to see her. I was disturbed by her wet clothes, her naked flesh beneath. I knew what people would say, and in spite of myself I sometimes wondered if they were right. She stood in front of me, breathless and laughing, shaking the water from her hair and wringing the hem of her shift between her hands.

'Aren't you cold?' I said. 'Do you want to borrow my cloak?'

'No, no, I'm not cold. I feel free, and new, and ready for anything.' Laughing, sparkling, frightening me with her daring. She took my face between her wet hands and kissed me. 'He says there's somebody else coming after him, somebody whose shoes he's not worthy to untie. What do you think he means?'

'I don't know. Some people say he's mad. I don't think you should take him too seriously.' She let go of my face and ran her fingers through her hair, irritated because I had said the wrong thing. Something about her infuriated me. I can't forgive myself for what I said next. 'Anyway Mary, why all the curiosity about yet another man? You already have two. Isn't that more than enough for any woman?' She narrowed her eyes and glared at me the way she used to. I waited for the furious response that would trigger a row between us, but eventually she just shrugged and turned away from me.

'Honestly Martha, I can't believe how dull life would be if we were all like you. You're so sensible.' Her voice was coldly dismissive.

'Well, somebody has to be sensible.'

'Why?'

'Well, because. Because otherwise, we'd all be like you.'

She raised her arms high above her head and clasped her hands, then she turned slowly to face me, confronting me with her beautiful body stretched out between heaven and earth. The wet coils of her hair snaked about her head and shoulders. She closed her eyes and tilted her face to the sky, and sunlight gilded her brow and her cheekbones. I was reminded of the goddesses that the pagans worship. I have never felt so lumpish and plain, nor have I ever felt such silent fury towards her.

I am never lost for words that express the small and insignificant details of life, but when feelings overwhelm me I drown in a sea of broken language. Mary thinks the insignificant things of life are not worth mentioning, but she can always find incantations for her magic and lamentations for her misery.

I stood there trapped in my body and watched as she shed her mortal flesh and became a shaft of light in the midday heat, her body spangling with the dewdrops of her baptism. Perhaps it is just as well that I had no words to say to her in that moment, for I would have killed her with my envy if I could have found the language to do it.

And then I saw that she had gooseflesh, and she was beginning to shiver, and she was no longer a goddess. She was my sister, my twin, flesh of my flesh, mirror to my being that reflected back my other self, my rampant and beautiful self that cowers in its pouch of womanliness and never dares to speak except through her. I wrapped my cloak around her like a mother indulging her rebellious daughter. She rolled her eyes, but she snuggled into it and I rubbed her shoulders through the cloth to warm her. Then she glanced up, and I followed her gaze.

A small group was coming towards us down the hillside. It was the time of year when the wilderness blooms, and the wild flowers sparkled and danced like a million jewels in the path of the man who led them. He walked with confidence, as if he owned the ground he walked on. And yet there was a loose and graceful freedom about him, so that arms and legs and air and flowers and sunlight were all part of one single flowing movement. He belonged to the earth, just as much as the earth belonged to him. There was a sudden stillness, such as I have never known before. The whole of creation seemed to be holding its breath, poised on the brink of something altogether strange and new.

John stood beside the river, watching. My sister was tense, alert, waiting for something to happen. When Mary has that air of expectancy about her, everything becomes charged with excitement. So it was that day, with some thrill of anticipation passing from the man in the river through my sister to the man on the hillside. I looked at her, and there was a pulse beating in a blue vein in her neck like a caged bird. The man walking down the hill seemed to walk to the rhythms of that pulse, as if all the cosmos was beating in time to my sister's heart.

I was suddenly afraid. I wanted to cover my face, to hide. I found myself repeating the words of the prophet Isaiah, but I did not know why. 'What a wretched state I am in! I am lost, for I am a woman of unclean lips and I live among a people of unclean lips, and my eyes have looked at the King, Yahweh Sabaoth.' What did it mean?

Only two years later did I remember those words, when he walked into Bethany after Lazarus had died. I watched him walking through the streets of the village with that same graceful presence, and in all my desolation and loss I suddenly recalled that day beside the Jordan and I knew, I knew what the words of the prophet meant. That was why I said what I did, when he asked me if I believed in him. 'I believe that you are the Christ, the Son of God, the one who was to come into this world.'

For the first time in my life, I knew that my words were important, that I had said something which escaped the confines of my daily world. But I did not really know the meaning of what I said, because it was a form of knowing that can't be called knowledge or understanding, a form of knowing that has no words or signs to express it, because it happens in the heart and not in the head.

Is that how Mary feels, I wonder, in those rapturous moments when her body melts and her spirit rests on the surface of her being?

And now he stand beside me in the kitchen, and I scold him because he picks and nibbles at the food I'm preparing, and he teases me because I fuss too much, and our gentle laughter hides the wells of sadness in our souls. He is like a little child, too innocent for this world. I long to wrap him in my arms and nestle him against my breast and rock backwards and forwards until he falls into a quiet sleep and escapes the cruel face that the world so often seems to turn towards him.

MARY

I stand in the kitchen doorway, watching the women at work. Martha is busy as ever, a mother hen who clucks and bustles through life. Mary the mother of Jesus stands a little apart, watching them with her back straight and her head held high. Elizabeth sits at the table, her body bent and gnarled like a tree that has grown in a barren and windswept place, mother of pain and the wilderness. She makes her younger cousin look ripe and fruitful, but Mary's fruitfulness is heavy tonight, as if the juices of suffering and surrender press against her skin and might burst forth upon us all. She exudes a sense of mysterious brooding, so that it seems as if the mood which overshadows the city tonight is an emanation of her own soul.

Jesus mirrors her posture, standing next to Martha and watching her work. Martha bastes the lamb and sprinkles it with herbs. He picks up the dough and pats the unleavened bread into shape, then he hands it to Martha and she puts it on a dish and slides it into the oven. She bends over and breathes in the smell of the red wine in the jug on the table. She smiles at Jesus, her sweet, motherly smile.

'I shall never drink good wine without remembering you,' she says. There is a stirring in the room, although nobody moves. Her words make eddies of sadness because they whisper of losses to come, and none of us dares to ask what she means. Jesus gazes at her in silence, and then he reaches out and runs the back of his hand down the side of her face. 'Thank you,' he murmurs. Then with that sudden explosion of movement which is so characteristic of him, he breaks the silence with a shout of laughter and flings his arms out wide.

The room is too small for such vast gestures. Some of the women step backwards out of his way. He throws his head back, and I feel his energy zing through the air. For a moment, I think that if we were not in this low-ceilinged room, he would burst through the layers of night and dance across the heavens to show us the joy of his being.

'Let's make it a night to remember. Come, let's eat, drink and be merry tonight.'

Nobody says 'for tomorrow we die.' Nobody says it, but I think everybody hears it anyway. He turns to look at me, and there is such ecstacy on his face that I feel my answering smile melt and slither across the room to stroke his skin. And overwhelmed, I need to escape, to be alone, to learn to breathe again.

'I'll call the servant for the washing of feet,' I say.

'I shall wash your feet tonight,' he says.

'Then I'll fetch the water.' I pick up a lamp and a jar to carry the water. I kick off my sandals to negotiate the smooth, uneven steps, and with the jar tucked onto my left hip I go down the stairs to the cistern under the house where water gathers from the intermittent rain which falls on the surrounding hills.

I go down to pools of darkness and secrets of night. I shall draw peace from the quiet waters that gather beyond the gaze of moonlight and stars.

The walls curve coldly above my head, like the contours of a womb turned to stone. I stroke the wall as I have stroked men's bodies in my desire, as I have stroked his body in undemanding love, speaking with my fingertips and tracing the shape of my devotion on his submissive flesh that gives and gives but asks nothing in return.

My lamp spreads a sheen of gold over the surface of the water, with a quivering jewel of light reflecting the flame. I bend over and dip my fingers in the water and feel the shiver up my arm. My touch fragments the smooth reflected glow and sends golden shards darting towards the walls. I swirl my hand and set in motion a frenzied, liquid dance of shadow and light, and I long for the freedom of the elements, for the leaping of the flame and the splash of the water and the serenity of the earth and the wild breath of the air.

Flesh and blood and limb fragment like lamplight on water. I am particles of being tossed on the memory of his laughter, and my spirit is swept up in that great movement of his head and his arms, and I hear a sound which I know is my own voice, and I wonder if I'm laughing or if I'm crying, but it is a voice that has no body and no meaning. Pure sound, pure liquid voice with the light of eternity sparking and glittering about it. Laughter, quickly followed by a grief that rips the air from my lungs.

I am buffetted, howling spirit tearing my limbs and shredding my muscles and turning my ligaments to froth. The curving walls of the cistern are pale as bone, a skull enclosing me in the empty socket of death. I am dissolving into the hours to come. I am in a vortex and it is too late to turn around. Tonight, the cosmos is consumed. Tonight, all time, all life, all past, all future, merge and dissolve into primal rage. And only his mother will truly remember how to love in the darkest of dark hours, and because she remembers, she will carry us in the womb of her grief and birth us anew on the far side of death.

My knees are weak and my legs are jelly. I slump against the wall and let my body slide to the ground. My head flops to one side and my breath heaves against my lungs. The water blurs in my vision and becomes the wilderness shimmering in the midday sun. Demons whisper their threats of terror and their promises of power. I see a man who struggles against them. I feel the barbs of his thirst in the back of my throat, and his hunger gnaws at my belly. I feel his desire for the glory and power of the world. I lie there for a moment, for an hour, for forty days and forty nights, for as long as it takes to feel as he felt, until I can no longer resist the leering seductions of the damned. Their wild shadows leap on the walls, fingers of darkness clawing at my gaze. Their moans rise from the depths of the pool, as if the dust of their bones and the rust of their blood has seeped into the water as it gurgled down the thirsty desert slopes, parodying the innocence of a baby's laugh. A silent howl deafens the ears of my soul, and I drown like a fish beached in the cruel air.

And then my vision focuses again, and the hazy wilderness rises in golden contours and shadows before my eyes. The air settles about me, consoling and sweet as a lover's breath. I can smell the familiar tang of his sweat, the dust of the day and the fragrance of dough still clinging to his hands as he crouches beside me. I lift my finger and trace the gentle rise of the hill where he fed five thousand and more hungry people. I run my fingernail down the narrow gulley where we walked late in the afternoon, and he spoke of the birds of the air and the lilies of the field. His bare foot beside my face becomes the landscape of our shared world. He has come down to find me. He did not forsake me in the wilderness of his pain.

He twines a strand of my hair around his fingers. I close my eyes and feel the healing in his touch. He cups his hand in the water and dribbles it over my forehead and neck. He takes another scoop of water and trickles it into my half open mouth, and the wine of his suffering and love burn my throat, so that I think of the wedding at Cana. I roll onto my back and gaze at him. I reach up and stroke the hair from his brow.

'Remember the wedding?' I say.

'I remember.'

'Your mother was so beautiful, like a bride.' How I loved her that day, with her imperious bearing and her strong commanding voice, and yet such youthfulness in her laughter and such delight in the sparkle of her eyes.

'You were all like brides that day.'

'And you? Who were you? Solomon?' I tease him with my smile.

'Why do you ask that? Because of my wisdom, perhaps?' He is teasing me too.

'No. Your abundance of brides. I should like to be your Bathsheba.'

'Bathsheba was Uriah's wife.'

'Every woman is allowed to make one mistake.'

'Like Eve?'

'Maybe. Have you ever made a mistake? Have you ever done something that you regret, or wish you could undo?'

'I should like to undo it all.'

'All?'

'Yes, all. The regrets, the mistakes, everything.'

'Everything? All the way back to Eve?'

'All the way back to Eve.'

I close my eyes and I imagine my sister naked in her garden of glory. How she longed to taste the fruit that was just out of reach, the one with the waxy red skin and the dew still fresh on its leaves. How daring was her desire. Other women want marriage, children, quiet lives, but Eve wanted the knowledge of God, and she would risk her very soul for that. While Adam slept, the woman stretched her arm above her head and plucked the fruit of her desiring from the tree of death. But she did not know, for how could she know the nature of evil and death, when she had not yet eaten the fruit? Innocent Eve, wanting the knowledge of good and evil, so that only with hindsight would she be able to tell the difference, and to know that her desire was not good.

But how could it be evil, until knowledge made it so? Ah, this knowledge kills us all. How I long not to know. To live in a world where we are free to be, free to desire, free to love, free from our deadly knowledge which judges and condemns. How terrible is our knowledge of God. What did Eve acquire on our behalf that day, when she bequeathed to us the legacy of her forbidden desire?

I look up at the man who kneels beside me, and I wonder if my desire for him is a desire for death or for life. They are so very close, sometimes I can hardly tell them apart. Is that what it means to lose Eve's knowledge, to regain innocence? Does it mean that it no longer matters, neither death nor life nor desire nor love nor good nor evil? An indifferent life in an indifferent world? No. If that is paradise, then better this nameless desire that is beyond good and evil but burns with a passion and a terror beyond all human knowing, so that it feels like the flame of God's love in the soul.

Lying here with my head resting on his legs, I think that I could reach up and pluck him from the air and he would be the fruit of my desiring, the fruit of my downfall or of my salvation, and only after I had eaten would I have the kind of knowledge that would enable me to tell the difference.

Then I remember what he called his mother that day. Woman. When she told him the wine was finished, he turned to her in bewilderment. 'Woman, what have I to do with you?'

The male disciples were troubled. Was Jesus publicly criticizing his mother? The law commands respect for one's mother and father. They huddled together, watching and muttering as is their habit when Jesus confuses them. I was more interested in Mary though. She held his gaze, as if his question lingered in the space between them and found its answer there. They no longer seemed like mother and son. They were lovers, but more ancient than the young lovers whose marriage we had come to celebrate. These two were bound together in some union more original than the flesh, more enduring than the marriage bond. But I also knew that this was a union that encompassed us all. Woman. Jesus had entered into a pact with woman that reached back to our mother Eve and made brides of us all.

Was it because Eve flinched in the end that her desire was cursed? Did some moment of doubt seize her at the very moment when she might have had what she longed for?

Mary did not flinch. She gazed unblinking at the angel, and said yes to the knowledge of God in her sinews and her flesh and her blood and her bone and her spirit and her desire. And that day at the wedding the scales fell from our eyes, and we stood for an instant with our primal parents beneath the tree of life, and we tasted the sweetness of love's fruit.

Didn't we know it? Didn't we sense that ripple of love among us, burning in our hearts as we watched the miracle unfold, and the servants pouring the wine, and the musicians beginning to play as musicians have never played before or since? While the men still huddled and mumbled in the corner, we women began to dance. Mary of Magdala, Mary Clopas, Mary Salome, Joanna, Ruth, Rachel, Leah, Rebecca, Naomi, Martha and I, Elizabeth, Mary his mother, Sarah the bride whose wedding we celebrated. We linked hands and we danced, and as we danced Jesus began to sing, and we wove our slow and graceful movements round the room to the sound of his voice. Dancing amidst and between us were our forgotten sisters with their laughter and tears. Sarah, Hagar, Judith, Bathsheba, Hannah, Peninnah, Adah, Zillah, Naamah and Eve.

I knew that the male disciples were scandalized, that they would take control of this moment and its meaning would be stolen from us, but I did not care. What mattered was the dancing, and the singing, and the wine that flowed so freely among the guests, and the smiles that we women exchanged one with another on that day when we were God's brides.

He stands up and pulls me to my feet, then he lifts my water jar and begins filling it. Together we climb the steps to the uneasy conversation of our friends and the soft light that holds back the waiting night.

The disciples have gathered in the room in readiness for our meal together. Jesus and I go into the kitchen to fetch a bowl and a towel for the washing of feet. Only Martha remains in the kitchen, busy with the final preparations.

I watch her as she arranges the lamb on a platter and garnishes it with herbs. Her face is attentive, as if she is performing some great work of art. A small frown wrinkles the bridge of her nose, and a strand of hair falls in front of her eyes, damp with sweat from the effort of her task. I am reminded of Jesus at his carpentry, for she wears the same look of absorption and peace. She steps back to survey her handiwork, and a smile of pleasure breaks over her face. She turns to us, eyes alight and face aglow with that quiet joy which seems so often to radiate from her now. I want to go and put my arms around her, but suddenly her expression changes. Jesus and I are standing with our backs to the door. She has seen something behind us, and her flushed cheeks fade to ash. My heart leaps within me, but I force myself to turn around.

STRUGGLE

MARTHA

Judas has staggered to the top of the stairs. Crimson saliva froths around his mouth, and blood blackens on his temple from a gash on his forehead. His tunic is torn and I can see the heaving of his naked chest. I think he's drunk. Before any of us knows what's happening, he lunges at Jesus and punches him in the face. Mary hurries to my side to get away from his flailing arms, and I wrap my arms protectively around her. He grips Jesus' shoulders, shaking him and shouting.

'Traitor!' he screams. 'Traitor! We followed you. We believed in you. For three years we've starved with you, wept with you, trampled the desert with you, waiting for the moment when the time was right. When? In the name of God, when will the time be right, Jesus? Our people are dying. Tonight, the Romans are prowling like vultures among us. I saw them out there, raping a woman while her little daughter stood watching and wailing. Is this your idea of the Kingdom of God? The women of Jerusalem, raped by Roman soldiers while you eat and drink with your friends in the privacy of a warm room. You have deceived us! It's your own vanity, that's all. You want attention, adoration, praise. You want love, when our people are starving and dying in the streets. You talk of the Kingdom of God? Come with me, now. Come out onto the streets where men are gathering and arming themselves in darkness. Come and fight for the people you claim to love. Take hold of the sword and show us your courage. Show us you're willing to die for what you believe!'

Blood seeps down Jesus' face from a graze on his cheekbone. His eye is bruised. As I watch, he raises his arms and grips Judas, just as Judas grips him. Mary tightens her hold on me, and instinctively we cling to one another as the two men begin a slow and monstrous wrestling, as if they are performing some strange rite of initiation. Judas rips away Jesus' robes, so that their naked torsos writhe and coil together like serpents. I cannot tell their limbs apart. Their shapes leap grotesquely on the walls, a two-headed monster of the shades locked in a battle against the light.

The others have heard the commotion, and they huddle around the doorway, watching, eyes wide with the dread of what we are witnessing. I catch John's eye, and I see desolation in his gaze so that I want to weep for all of us. Quiet, gentle John, companion to Jesus in a way that is less demanding than the companionship of my sister, more spiritual than my earthy love. I think that no matter what happens, John will always be loyal to Jesus, but tonight I see that his heart is breaking.

We women are not the only ones to suffer at the hands of the Romans. We found John in the gutter one night when we were returning to our home in Bethany. My sister and I had invited some of the disciples for a meal. There was Jesus, Peter, Bartholomew, Thomas, Rachel, Rebecca, and Mary of Magdala. John had been raped and left for dead by the Romans.

Peter urged Jesus to leave him there, naked and dying in the ditch, for surely he was guilty of the sin of Sodom and his flesh was unclean and untouchable. But

Jesus climbed down beside John, and he covered his nakedness with his cloak, and with the hem of his robe he began to wipe the blood and the semen from John's body. I went to help him, and together we made strips from my skirt to bandage his wounds, and then we carried him back to our house in Bethany, where I tended his wounds until he was strong enough to accompany us on short journeys.

John still limps and he has lost the use of one arm. His soul bleeds like a woman's body, because John now shares our womanliness. That's why the men avoid him and turn away in disgust when Jesus holds him and soothes him and restores the touch of tender loving to his flesh.

'Turn the other cheek.' Again and again, Jesus has warned us against retaliation, against violence. 'Do not be afraid of those who destroy the body.' If the rest of us are sometimes unconvinced, sometimes confused about this message of peace and reconciliation even with our enemies, John never wavers. He is convinced to the depth of his being that what Jesus says has some ultimate truth about it, and tonight I see that his faith is being tested to breaking point. For John, it is impossible that Jesus would use violence against Judas, impossible that Jesus would in the end be as weak as other men in his convictions. So I see in John's eyes an inability to believe what he sees, a refusal to accept the meaning of this for us all.

I am suddenly aghast at the violence men do to each other. John, broken and wounded in body and soul. Judas, with a hatred that gnaws at his spirit. And now even Jesus, bleeding and battered and unable in the end to resist becoming part of it, unable to resist the violence of men.

He is struggling for his life, but the method of his struggle will surely destroy us, for if he kills Judas then he betrays everything he represents for those of us who follow him. If we had wanted to follow one who will kill in self-defence, we would have followed Judas, not Jesus. Perhaps they are one and the same after all, and in the killing of Judas we will see the unmasking of Jesus. God have mercy on us all.

MARY

I am sick with dread, but I am caught in the grip of some bleak fascination. Is this the moment I have been afraid of? If Judas kills Jesus, will I love him even in death? Or do I love him only because I believe him to be invincible? And what if Jesus kills Judas, what then? Will I love him with blood on his hands? What is it I love in him? Is it death, or is it life? I feel as if my spirit has been hurled into the fight with them, so that I am beaten and torn between them.

But as I watch, something happens to the shape and the mood of their struggle. They begin to make huge circling movements, locked in one another's arms, swaying and undulating with a unity of purpose that is incomprehensible to the rest of us. Even lovers in their greatest passion do not achieve this harmony between two bodies. Slowly, quietly, they subside into stillness, and Judas puts his head on Jesus' shoulder and sobs as I have never heard a man sob before. Not even Lazarus, fresh from the horror of the grave, sobbed like that.

'Judas, Judas,' says Jesus, and cupping Judas' face in his hands he raises his head so that their eyes meet. 'What have you to do with me?' he says.

I am reminded of his mother, and I search for her among the pale and silent faces in the doorway. She is there among them, her eyes darkened with something beyond fear and grief, as if she sees into realms that are hidden to the rest of us. Sometimes she terrifies me, this woman of the rocky countenance and the shadowed gaze. I turn away, unable to contemplate her dark wisdom.

MARTHA

Jesus is pale and bruised, breathless from their struggle, but he looks at him with tender bewilderment. 'Judas, Judas, what have you to do with me?'

Judas is a man in torment. His mouth is contorted with grief and his eyes blaze with fury and terror.

'I don't know. Tell me, what have I to do with you?' he wails. 'They were taunting me, urging me to leave you and fight with them. That's why the fight started. Help me, please help me. My Lord, help me.'

He falls to his knees and wraps his arms around Jesus' legs. Jesus extricates himself and pours some water into the bowl. His palms bear the marks of Judas' blood. He takes the towel and kneels down beside Judas. He washes his bloodstained hands, and then he dips a corner of the towel into the water and gently wipes away the blood from Judas' face.

'Judas, you must do what you have to do,' he whispers.

They kneel face to face, staring at each other, and then Jesus leans forward and kisses Judas on the lips. Blood trickles down Jesus' face from the graze on his cheek, and it leaves a mark on Judas' lips. I go and take the towel from Jesus, and kneeling beside them I wipe his face as he has just wiped Judas' face. I squeeze the towel in the water, and it reddens with the mingling of their blood. Jesus stands up, ties the towel around his waist and picks up the water bowl.

'Come,' he says, 'we must wash our feet and begin our meal.'

ENCOUNTER

MARTHA

We arrange ourselves around the table, and on every face there are the same furrows of stress framing the smiles of our friendship. This is our third seder together, the third year when we have gathered for the passover to share a meal and pray and sing praise to the Lord for delivering us out of the land of Egypt. I have set out the meal carefully in its proper order, each portion reminding us of some aspect of our people's suffering and deliverance. The bitter herbs and the bread of our affliction, the four cups of wine for each of us, to remind us of our joy as well as our grief. Only at the end will I bring in the lamb, after we have eaten everything else. Our rabbis tell us that we must eat the lamb last, so that its taste will remain in our mouths.

Judas is sitting next to me, with his face battered and his clothes torn. I scarcely recognize the man I once knew, powerful, impressive, majestic in his convictions and his passions.

Mary and I first went to hear him speaking soon after our parents died. I think we had secret dreams of carrying on the work of our father, more in honour of his memory than because of any commitment to his cause. Our mother used to smile indulgently when he talked about liberating the Jewish people from the Roman empire. 'Jacob, Jacob, we are so small and helpless. Look at the Romans with their armies and their weapons and their chariots. Come now, be thankful that we have food to eat and two fine daughters to bless our marriage. That is enough for us. We should thank God that we have quiet lives. If we don't bother the Romans, they won't bother us.'

But my father did bother the Romans, although he was a small, shy man and surely could have done them no harm. He attended meetings and liked to listen to great speakers, sheltering in the aura of their courage. He had been to listen to Judas the day he died. It was because he went to hear Judas that they killed him.

The Romans were afraid of Judas. Crowds were beginning to follow him. After one of his speeches there was an uprising and a Roman soldier was killed in the streets of Jerusalem. My father had come straight home to Bethany and knew nothing of the troubles, but somebody told the soldiers that he had been at the gathering, and that's why they came looking for him.

It was my mother, not my father, who shouted abuse and told them to leave us alone. So they killed her as well as him, and Mary and I became orphans in a strange world, with our womanhood budding on our breasts and the bloody promises of motherhood beginning to leak from our bodies.

In the defiant passion of our grief we started to follow Judas. We had nothing to lose, and if the soldiers killed us too then it would be blessed relief from the anguish of living. We stayed on in our parents' house, although it was a haunted place with a bloodstained floor that daily taunted us with the image of their dying.

One night, there was a knock on the door when we were in bed. Mary and I shared a bed after they died, because we needed one another's warmth in the dark hours when death lurked in our nightmares. I wanted to ignore the person at the door. So often we told

71

ourselves that we were not afraid of dying, that we would welcome the sword that would take us to join our parents, but it wasn't true. That night, imagining the soldier or the rapist or the robber, I did not want to greet death on the doorstep. I wanted to hide in our warm bed, because although our hearts were broken still they beat with the hopefulness of life, and I wanted to live.

I turned to look at my sister. Her eyes were fierce and her face was pale amidst the wild froth of her hair. When Mary looks like that, she terrifies me more than death. She is fearless, as if she would defy even the powers of hell.

'Stay here,' I begged her. 'If we ignore them, they might go away.'

'What if it's somebody in trouble?' she said, although in truth it would be me, not Mary, who would worry about that. My sister has a loving heart, but sometimes she shows a strange indifference to weakness and suffering. Deep down, I think she despises those of us who lack her fighting spirit.

I sat nervously beside her, holding my breath and straining my ears for every sound, trying to picture who it might be. Was it a woman or even a child, attacked and abandoned in the street? The knocking came again, a light tapping as if the person was afraid of being heard.

Mary climbed out of bed and wrapped her cloak about her. I had to let her go. I remembered the story in the scriptures, of the Levite's concubine who was attacked by the men of Gibeah. In the morning she lay dying with her hands on the threshhold of her host's door. I imagined opening the door in the morning and finding the body of the unnamed woman who had come to us for help, and I found no answer. In spite of my fear, I was glad that Mary opened the door.

MARY

That night I fell in love for the first but not the only time in my life. I stood behind the door and called to the unseen presence on the other side.

'Who is it?'

'It's me, Judas. I need shelter for the night. The Romans are looking for me.'

The Romans were our enemies. They had killed our parents, and Judas' angry rhetoric had persuaded Martha and me that we must dedicate our lives to the struggle for freedom. I felt joyful terror at the thought of helping Judas, at the thought of hiding him in our home and offering him refuge from the soldiers who daily clattered along the cobblestones on the road outside, leering at Martha and me when we went to the well and calling out their lewd remarks as we walked past. Judas offered vengeance, and I wanted vengeance.

While Martha prepared a meal, I washed the dust of the wilderness from his feet, and it was then that I first felt the fire in my soul and the hunger in my body. I had washed men's feet before, but never had I been so conscious of the touch and the smell and the strength of a man's body. I lingered over the task, savouring the tender flesh, the tufts of hair on his toes, the callouses on his heels. I was innocent of men's desires and dreams, oblivious to the power of my fingertips. When I felt his hands in my hair, loosening the clasps and letting it fall about my shoulders, I was not ashamed. I raised my face to his and I was surprised by the intensity of his gaze, but I did not look away.

I sat with Judas after Martha was in bed. As he spoke, the lamplight carved deep shadows on his face and turned his eyes into burning coals. I was captivated by the ripple of his skin and the curves of his body as he lounged on the floor, speaking of resistance and struggle and freedom.

When eventually I left him and crawled quietly into bed beside Martha, I could not sleep. I lay on my back watching the moonlight feathering the walls, listening to the ripple of her breath in the night. For the first time since our parents died, I thought of the future and not of the past. I had a sense of standing on the edge of time, as if the story of my life was about to begin. I felt the stroke of desire on my flesh, and a sweet thickening in my throat as if the air I breathed had turned to honey. I translated these strange sensations into girlish dreams that I could understand. I told myself that I would marry Judas and together we would change the world.

I fell asleep as the dawn dribbled through the window and made puddles of light on my sister's face. When we awoke, Judas had gone. That day, the Romans heard that we had sheltered him during the night, and they came and destroyed our house. I was secretly glad to see the shattered walls bury the stain of our parents' death, even if it meant that Martha and I had no home.

We did not see Judas again for four years. We heard he was in hiding, but we did not know where. When he reappeared in our lives my brief marriage was over and Lazarus was sharing my bed.

We met up with Judas in a crowd, gathered around a new teacher who stood on a hillside and spoke as Judas used to, but the words he used and the vision that inspired him were such as we had never encountered before. 'Happy the gentle. They shall have the earth for their heritage. Happy those who mourn. They shall be comforted.'

That was a few days after my baptism in the river Jordan. I recognized this teacher. He was the man who was baptized after me, a second cousin of John the Baptist. My senses were heightened that day of my baptism, by the water and the breeze on my skin and some strange sense of newness in my heart. The lazy river meandered through a carpet of flowers, and the wild man of God stood up to his waist in the water and watched as Jesus approached. He splashed into the river with the enthusiasm of a little child, startling a flock of doves in the trees nearby so that they swirled up against the blue sky like a handful of promises tossed up from earth to heaven. It was a moment I would not forget.

And then I heard him speaking a few days later, and I knew that I had met somebody greater than Judas. I went home and called Lazarus and my sister, and we have followed him ever since.

MARTHA

That day, Jesus' voice filled the valley, so that the stones seemed to take up his message and play with the echo of his words. There was a new mood among the crowds, not the restless fury that Judas used to inspire, which made men clench their fists and punch the air and made women urge their sons to join the struggle. When Jesus spoke there was joy and laughter among the people. Strangers chatted together like old friends. Those who had food shared with those who had none, creating a miraculous abundance out of small offerings of bread. We discovered a freedom within our own hearts, a freedom that brought peace and compassion to our lives. Instead of throwing stones at the soldiers and shouting abuse we began to greet them in the streets and invite them into our homes. We discovered that if we were too small and helpless to win our freedom through violence we might achieve an even greater freedom through love.

Even Judas was persuaded, at first. I don't believe he ever wanted violence and bloodshed. He was a man consumed by righteous anger, a man who could not sit back and watch the oppression of the weak by the powerful, a man compelled to act by the sight of our people's pain. But I think he was also tired of the fighting and the struggle, tired of being hunted, tired of failure. Jesus suggested a different approach. We could not conquer our enemies by force, but perhaps we could love them into submission.

And now, tonight, they sit at a table together, bearing the wounds of their struggle, and Judas watches Jesus with a darkness that I have never seen before. He is like some great beast wounded in the struggle for survival. I long to comfort him, but I'm also afraid of him.

Perhaps he's right. We are weak and cowardly. We should not be here celebrating in a quiet room, when outside there's menace and terror on the streets. Really, when all is said and done, why do our people offer such lavish praise for such frugal blessings? Judas senses me watching him and seems to read my thoughts.

'The night of our deliverance, eh, Martha? Thanks be to God.' There's a sourness in his voice as if his dreams have turned rancid.

'It is the night of our deliverance, Judas. We must not lose faith.' He sneers at me.

'Good faithful Martha. Always following the rules. Doing what she's told. Don't you ever want to cry out, Martha? For God's sake, don't you ever think for yourself?' I feel the pain of an ancient wound reopening. Dull, stupid Martha, always imitating somebody else, usually her sister, never having a thought of her own, an idea worth sharing, a comment worth repeating. Perhaps I'm over-tired. Maybe their strain has communicated itself to me, in spite of the food and the preparation and the joy I felt in the kitchen. I am aware of a weight on my soul, and my voice seems to ooze thickly through the lamplight when I speak.

'Yes, Judas, yes, I do think for myself. Do you want to know what I think?' I try to stare him down. He shrugs and averts his eyes.

'I'm going to tell you anyway, Judas. I'm going to tell you what I think. Sometimes I wonder what kind

The Last Supper according to Martha and Mary

of deliverance we're talking about. I find it difficult not
to ask such questions when I think of my mother and
the look in her eyes when she died. She died as
someone betrayed by God, do you know that Judas?
Do you know what that means, to faithful people like
my parents? To die abandoned by God? There's
nothing worse Judas. I carry the scorch marks of my
mother's dying look on my soul. And then I think that
they were only two among hundreds of thousands.
Before the Romans it was the Greeks, and before them
it was the Persians, and before them it was the
Egyptians, and after the Romans there will be
somebody else, some new empire, some new belief,
some new reason for killing and for dying. And when
men like you, and like him'—I flick my hand at Jesus,
standing nearby preparing to wash our feet—'finish
your preaching and your shouting, it's left to the
women to mop up the blood and anoint the bodies.'

'Martha . . .'

'Don't interrupt me, Judas, I'm not finished yet. You
wanted to know what I think, and I'm telling you.
Today, I was following Jesus at a distance, talking to a
woman in the crowd. Her husband had died many
years ago. Her eldest son was sick, and she thought he
too was dying, and she had come looking for Jesus,
because she had heard that he had the gift of healing,
and she thought that if he would come and visit her
son perhaps he would heal him, because if her son
dies, Judas, she will have no breadwinner in her family.
She must feed her other children and the only way she
can do that is to sell her daughter's body to the Roman
soldiers. So she came, but there were too many people

and she couldn't get near Jesus, so she went home saying that she would try again tomorrow, but her son is very ill, he might not survive the night, and she's just one among so many, so many. And I ask myself, did our mothers bury their stillborn infants in the desert and endure the hunger and thirst of their children for this? Is this what God means by deliverance? Yes, Judas, God help us.'

'I have a dream, Martha . . .'

'So do I, Judas. Sometimes, when we all walk with Jesus late in the afternoon, when the sun's going down and you can almost feel God's breath in the air, and we've had a good day and we feel warm and close, sometimes then I also have a dream. I dream that we're real, that what we're doing is real. This is it. This is what it's all about. This is what we've been waiting for. That's my dream, Judas. That's when I really do believe that this is the promised land that our mothers dreamed of.

'But so often there's only the wilderness and the rocks and the barren sand, and I feel the sun shrivelling our dreams and laying them waste in the desert, and God's love is as harsh and cruel as the sun itself. He made other creatures more able to endure this place than us, but he gave us no armoured shell, no spirit of indifference to gaze unblinking on each other's pain. Our skin is too soft and our hearts are too tender for this land the Lord has given us, for the grief of being his people. He gave us minds and imaginations to inhabit each other's lives, and sometimes I think our collective pain acccumulates within us until our spirits will fall apart under the burden.' The words tumble from me with an eloquence that surely isn't my own. I am breathless, exhilarated, shocked. My face is burning. He stares at me in silence. I dare to glance across at Jesus, and he too is watching me. Embarassed, I shrug and try to laugh. 'There,' I say, 'that's what I think. You did ask me.'

Judas grasps my arm and puts his face very close to mine so that I can smell his drunkenness on his breath. 'Come away with me, Martha,' he whispers. 'Let's start again. There's still time. We can make it happen. We can change the world.' Once, his eyes burned with the power of his vision. Now, I gaze at the empty stare of a man demented with failure. I shake my head.

'Ah no, Judas. You would achieve your dreams with the sword, and always there would be an army with more swords, an empire with stronger men, don't you see?' I try to rest my hand on his arm to placate him, but he shakes me off angrily.

'Only because we follow the wrong people. We're always seduced by the foolish promises of the weak.' He is glaring at Jesus, so that I am suddenly terrified in case he hits him again. What madness is there among us tonight? It's as if all the forces of destruction are battering against our fragile souls. How exhausted we are. How much longer can this continue? I am drained of words, drained of gestures. I should like to rest my head on my arms and sleep. Jesus reaches across the table and takes my hand.

'Be brave, Martha. Soon you will have to carry all their burdens.'

'What do you mean?'

'Shhh. The time has nearly come. We must begin.'

COMMUNION

MARTHA

Jesus picks up the bowl of bloodied water and he kneels down to wash our feet, assuming the role of a servant. He goes to Thomas first, and Thomas recoils.

'What are you doing, Jesus? How can you wash us in blood? We will be impure. Why don't you tell one of the women to fetch clean water?'

'How often have I told you, Thomas? Nothing on the outside can make you impure. It's what's in your heart that matters.'

Thomas hesitates, foot poised above the bowl, doubt in his eyes. Then slowly, as if he is condemning himself, he allows Jesus to trickle the water onto his skin and and the grime of the desert mingles with the bloodied water.

Next Jesus goes to Ruth. Her large belly makes her movements awkward, and they laugh together as she struggles to lift her feet and then drops them clumsily into the bowl so that she splashes his face and his clothes. Ruth's ankles are swollen, and I see how gently he massages them until her skin glows with his touch. Their laughing faces comfort me. I feel the warmth and the words returning. I want to make light of my outburst, to laugh it away so that I don't have to think about what I said.

Veronica, sitting next to Ruth, takes her napkin and wipes the water from Jesus' face, and she too is laughing. Veronica is quiet, with a gentleness that attracts me. Like me, she's someone whose satisfaction comes from responding to the needs of others. But while I am always busy and like to be active, Veronica watches and waits in silence, and it is the need perceived by nobody else, the small grief or the small cry that gets drowned in the hubbub of our lives, that Veronica notices and responds to.

Mary of Magdala is next. She laughs nervously, and her hands flutter in the air like butterflies with broken wings. Mary's demons have left her, but sometimes it seems as if now she is inhabited by other spirits, spirits that do not howl with the madness of the past, but that gust through her soul with strange whispers and promises. She speaks and moves with such fragile grace that it seems as if she is more air than body, more breath than flesh. She is wearing a white dress, and as he kneels at her feet he seems caught up in the cloud of her presence. They are beautiful together, with an other-worldly beauty that makes me suddenly afraid. I long for this night to be over. Never have I felt so many emotions flooding through me at once.

Jesus goes to Joanna, then to Mary his mother. I wonder if this is the first time that a son has kneeled before his mother to wash her feet. Mary's foot snuggles against the palm of his hand, and they are sculpted from the same flesh and bone. She gazes down at him, and there is such an enormity of tenderness and grief in her eyes that I cannot bear to watch. It is as if she begins to feel a sword piercing her soul, and she bleeds in some mysterious abyss which is the depth of her love for him.

He goes to Mark and Andrew and then to Elizabeth, whose bent old feet resting in his hands look like the shrivelled remains of creatures that have died in the desert. He washes the feet of James and Rachel, and then he goes to Peter.

Peter stands up as Jesus approaches.

'Never!' he says. 'You shall never wash my feet.' Jesus kneels at his feet, gazing up at him. Peter draws his shoulders back defiantly. 'You are our master and our lord,' he says. 'You humiliate us by this behaviour.'

Poor Peter. He is always so concerned to preserve the order of things. I think he secretly admires the Romans and longs to be one of them with their ranks and their hierarchies and their emperors. Everybody has a rightful place, a role to play, and a duty to perform that tells them who they are. Peter is a fisherman who dreams of being a prince.

We are such daydreamers, all of us. We have such delusions of grandeur. Carving a life out of nothing and telling ourselves that we are the chosen ones of God.

Sometimes I wonder what inspired Peter to leave his nets and follow Jesus. I think he has suffered and struggled more than any of us to let go of the old ways, to let his spirit dance to the wild and wayward music of the wind. Jesus invites us to explore the secret patterns of God's world, to take the sun as our brother and the moon as our sister, to learn from the lilies of the field and the birds of the air. But Peter clings to the order that men impose on the world, and now he glares down at Jesus and his body refuses to yield.

MARY

Slowly, Jesus rises to his feet so that he gazes into Peter's eyes. Jesus is as tall as Peter, his shoulders as broad and his back as straight, but there is a difference in the shapes they make.

Their bodies carve a tableau before my eyes. Peter becomes chiselled in stone, conquering the space he occupies, his contours harsh against the gentle light. Jesus befriends the space, gathers it into himself, and the light itself takes shape in him and blurs the edges of presence and absence, of being and not being. And then it is as if Jesus begins to dissolve in the light, and his body melts so that eventually he is nothing but a faint glow radiating its warmth before the cold, hard statue of Peter. I want to call out to him to stay, not to leave us alone, not to disappear before Peter's frozen gaze, but my tongue is trapped in my mouth and my body is as rigid as Peter's.

'If I do not wash you, Peter, you can have nothing in common with me.' Jesus' voice breaks the spell, and Peter looks suddenly confused and disorientated. He hesitates, seems to debate with himself, and then he laughs. Just sometimes, Peter relaxes enough to let us see his sense of humour. I wish he did it more often, this proud, impetuous man who seems to have such a special place in Jesus' heart.

'Then not just my feet, but my hands and my head as well,' he says, and he plunges his hands into the water and splashes it over his hair and his beard like a little child. For a moment our fears are forgotten, as the two of them splash and laugh and frolic together.

In a sudden rush of embarassed affection, Peter looks at Jesus and says,

'I'll never leave you Lord, never.' Jesus rests his hand on Peter's shoulder.

'Before tonight is over, you will deny me three times,' he says.

The last traces of their laughter curdle in our ears. What does he mean? What does any of this mean? I feel as if we are caught in some mighty whirlwind, with the power to sweep us up in the exhilaration of faith, and to dash our spirits on the rocks of despair.

And now, at last, Jesus kneels at my feet. I have been washing men's feet since childhood, but never before has a man washed my feet. The lamplight makes a haze around his head as he bows in front of me. My foot looks small in his hand, and he touches me as if I were a newborn baby.

Is this a secret ritual that we share, he and I? Caught up in the swirl of memories, I think of that other night when I washed his feet, and the moment is suffused with an intimacy more profound than any I have known when lying naked in a man's arms. He and I are one, his skin on mine, the stroke of his fingers on my flesh, the warmth of the water seeping up through my body. I remember the smell of the perfume I used to anoint him, and I close my eyes and it is as if the fragrance still lingers between us and enfolds us like a lover's embrace.

But wasn't that the anointing of death? He spoke of the tomb, not of the marriage chamber, that night.

I open my eyes, and my gaze is drawn to Judas. That night when I anointed Jesus, Judas protested and said that the money should have been given to the poor. But Judas would have used that money to buy swords, not bread. Now he watches Jesus with despair in his eyes, and I feel as if I am gazing into the face of death itself.

I cannot look away. He looks up and catches me staring at him. He does not avert his eyes but holds my gaze. I feel as if he is sucking my soul from my body, draining me of life and energy, inviting me to join him in some godforsaken realm of betrayal and torment.

I force myself to look away. I try to focus again on Jesus, on his touch and his shape and the warm familiar smell of bread and sweat that clings to his body. But all I can smell is the sickly sweetness of blood and the musk of my own fear. On impulse, I lean forward and rest my hand on Jesus' head.

'Be careful,' I say.

He looks up, and I see my dread reflected in his eyes. I want him to comfort and reassure me. I want him to tell me that my fears are unfounded. Why does he look at me in that way? He is invincible. Nothing will ever harm him or destroy him. He is the Son of God.

No. No, that's not true. Martha said that in a moment of madness, but surely it's not true. It is blasphemy to say that. I don't want this beautiful man at my feet to bear the weight of the divine. I want to revel in his humanity. I want to love him and live with him and lie with him, not as the goddesses lie with their gods, but as a woman lies with a man, and gasps and weeps with the joy of their loving, and grows heavy with his children, and shares his youth and his age, his living and his dying. He is too young to die. He has scarcely lived.

But why do I think of dying at all? We are here to celebrate the passover, and tomorrow we will go to the temple for the sacrifice. After that, Martha and I will return to Bethany, and our lives will go on, surely?

Jesus looks at Judas and sees his despair, and a silent scream shreds the air between them.

MARY

The wine is like blood in the candlelight. The warm bread wraps us in its fragrance and reminds me of my mother's body when we were children and she held us in her arms. My mother was large and soft and comforting. How I miss her.

'This is my body.' My body. My body. What blessing is this? The words echo in my soul. He breaks the bread, and somewhere inside me I feel something breaking as well. We pass the bread around the table, and it rests drily on my tongue. I taste the wilderness, the dry years ahead.

'This is my blood.' The red wine glowers and throws its reflection on his face as he lifts the goblet to his lips. I think of my parents' blood, innocent ones killed for reasons they did not understand. I think of the mingling of blood in the bowl that we used for the washing of feet, blood spilled in the violence of love turned to hatred, and friendship to betrayal. Then I think of the fertile blood that flows from my body, weeping for the broken promise of the child that never comes, mourning for the men I never loved enough to make me want to bear their children.

Jesus takes a piece of bread and dips it into the wine. What is he doing? He gazes at Judas, and I see that his fear has turned to resignation. He reaches out and rests his hand for a moment on the top of Judas' head as if in blessing, and then he passes him the bread.

'Go quickly,' he says.

Judas takes the bread and eats it, and then he looks once more at Jesus as if appealing to him for something. For a moment he seems lost and afraid, like a child, and then his face clouds over and he stands up. His movement stirs the air, guttering the flame of the lamp so that the shadows dance on the walls like the beating wings of the angels of death that pass over our land. Then he is gone, and the night rushes in to fill the space of his absence.

HEALING

MARTHA

We sit in fretful silence, and the darkness snarls at us through the window. The voices that drift up from the streets are not the festive voices of our people gathering for the passover. They are threaded through with tension and fear. Sometimes I am amazed at how quickly the mood changes in this city. It is as if here we gather in all the threads of joy and sadness, hope and despair that weave together human destinies and make out of them a picture that changes even as we gaze at it, so that we never quite understand, we never grasp what this city is trying to tell us. Last week the people were in high spirits, and when Jesus entered the city they waved palm branches to greet him.

How absurd he looked. His huge body which looks as if it was made to sit on Solomon's throne, hunched ungainly on a donkey's back, and the people singing and cheering and rushing to touch him as if he really were Solomon in all his splendour. We were laughing, all of us, Jesus too. He takes our world and shakes it until words and meanings leave their neatly ordered ranks and spangle and dance in the breath of his being. He creates a world ruled by a king on a donkey, a world where a camel can pass through the eye of a needle and a blind man can gaze on the face of his daughter for the very first time, a world where Lazarus, dear beloved Lazarus, walks unharmed from the tomb, and where womanly life is restored to the one who has bled in untouchable shame for most of her adult life.

Naomi's husband left because he could not bear her
bloodied bed. She had long forgotten the loving touch
of a body that hungered for hers. In the first year of
her marriage she had given birth to a child, a daughter,
who whimpered and died on the birthing bed, and
Naomi's body had wept tears of blood ever since,
refusing to be consoled, repelling the fertile promise of
loving and birthing again. Until one day a man in a
crowd became the shape of her hope, and without
thinking, without knowing what made her do it, she
bent down and touched the hem of his cloak.

He turned. 'Who touched me?' he asked. I was
aghast. I could not understand why Jesus would
humiliate a woman in that way. When my sister was
dragged naked before him, he bent and wrote on the
ground so that she would not have the shame of
another man staring at her. Afterwards, we realized
what he had been writing. They were men's names, the
name of every man in the crowd who had committed
adultery. The list was long. So I could not understand
why Jesus wanted to shame Naomi in public, when he
had been so sensitive to my sister's shame.

Naomi recoiled and hung back in the crowd. The
people jostled her, and someone pushed her roughly.
The disciples had not noticed Naomi's gesture, and
they tried to tell Jesus it was just the crowds milling
around him. People are always reaching out to touch
Jesus. I wondered why he was making such a thing of
it.

'I felt the power go out of me,' he said. We women
knew about Naomi's bleeding body. We know how
afraid men are of the mysterious power of a woman

who is bleeding. When men bleed it always signifies wounding and pain. They do not know how to decipher the complex promises and threats of women's blood, so they shun us when we bleed and refuse to share our beds, to eat the food we prepare, to touch our flesh.

All this I knew, but I felt something sinking within me, a sense of disappointment in Jesus. He was, after all, just the same as the rest. Afraid of the bleeding woman and the threat she posed to his power.

I saw Naomi's body hunch over in shame. Women like Rachel and my sister face men with fury and fire to match their power, but Naomi was used to being rejected and despised, and she had forgotten how to stand tall and defend herself. So she shuffled towards Jesus with her head hung low and then she flung herself in the dust at his feet. Sobbing, she told him of the long years of bleeding and untouchability, of her loneliness and her longing, of the hunger of her flesh, but more, of the hunger of her heart for love and companionship. The women gasped and muttered among themselves. The men furrowed their brows and shook their heads at her lack of public decency.

Jesus knelt on the ground and took Naomi in his arms. The men beside me growled their indignation. She was untouchable. She was impure. What was he doing? Jesus held her until she was quiet, and then gently he raised her to her feet. She lifted her tear-stained face to his and gazed at him in amazement, and her smile was like a benediction on him.

'I'm no longer bleeding,' she said. 'I felt it. The moment I touched you, I felt that something had changed. You've healed me.'

'No Naomi, not I. It was your own faith that healed you. Now go in peace.'

Naomi was restored to strength in spirit as well as in body when she stood before us and declared herself healed. She no longer had anything to be ashamed of. Jesus had touched her and embraced her publicly, and in that gesture he put the men around him to shame and gave some new and unvoiced hope to the women. He seemed to be saying that our bodies are acceptable even when they bleed, even when men declare us unclean. I think that if Naomi had gone away believing that Jesus did not know she had touched him, her shame would have been greater, not less. That is what these rules do to women. If we touch a man when we are impure, we bear the guilt of defiling him. Naomi's body would have been healed, but the burden on her spirit would have been increased if Jesus had not acknowledged her touch.

Naomi has another daughter now, Hannah, two years old, a bright child who travels with us and delights us with her chatter and her games. We are a strange group. No wonder people stare. Fishermen and tax collectors, prostitutes and village women tired of the daily routine of life, children conceived in marriage beds and brothels, in quiet shadows late at night when most of the disciples are asleep, and a man and woman seek each other out and let their bodies speak the love that Jesus offers.

Like the women whose bellies grow big with their babies, we are bringing something living and new to the world, but I am afraid for what we are birthing. The world isn't ready for this. They do not want a king on a donkey, enemies turning the other cheek, love instead of hatred. That's why, this week, their songs and their praises have turned to sneers and hisses and taunts. Wherever we went today, it was the same. People huddled in doorways, watching, muttering, feeling some enormous, intangible sense of betrayal because whatever they were hoping for last week has not happened.

I think that even though he rode on a donkey they did not understand. They thought he was a king come to liberate his people. They thought the donkey was a joke—he has a sense of humour, they know that. They could not see that the donkey defined him, that the mute little beast with its gentle eyes was a sign of the utmost importance, however much the man on its back laughed. He was laughing as a small child laughs, a stranger to vanity and wounded pride, laughing because from the back of a donkey he looked at the world and saw its beauty, and maybe for a moment he believed that they saw it too. Maybe he believed that they sang and praised God because their eyes had been opened and they saw that the way to the kingdom was unfolding before them, in the laughter of a king who rode on a donkey.

But not so. And now he sits at table, and I see from the stoop of his shoulders that the spirit has gone from him. Judas has stolen something, taken it away into the night, and he does not know how to reclaim it. Perhaps he does not know if he wants to reclaim it. And looking round, I realize how dependent everybody is on him. It's as if they are falling apart, each lost in his or her own world, unable to reach out, to touch one another, to meet one another's eyes.

Then, quietly, his mother takes charge.

'Come Martha, let's bring the lamb,' she says. I am glad that I can make myself busy, that I can leave this room with its aura of dread and escape to the warmth of the kitchen. But I am glad too that I can bring my offering to the table, a shared meal that might yet have the power to gather us together in friendship beyond the bonds that have been broken tonight.

MARY

His mother sits across the table from me as we eat, and I marvel at her composure. Tonight, with darkness billowing around us, her presence takes on the form of a mighty suffering calm. She is beautiful in her ageing, this peasant woman with the regal gaze. She looks at her son who sits beside me, and their eyes meet across the table. I do not understand the relationship between these two, this loving desire that is too subtle and too mysterious to name. It is beyond the clumsy concepts of love and desire to which language gives voice. And yet it began only with voice and song, the voices of women and angels. Where were the men and the fathers?

Mary sometimes speaks of that day when she went to the well, lost in the sunlit beauty of the morning. She was a young village girl, engaged to be married to Joseph, living at home with her parents. Yet when Mary speaks about that time, her language is not that of the ordinary world she describes. She speaks of longing and dreams, of a boundless joy that spilled over and would not be contained. While the girls around her chattered about marriage and babies, homes and families, Mary could find no words to express her ecstatic emptiness. She loved Joseph, but he was not, and never would be, the desire of her heart. She would not serve him, bear his children and wait upon his needs. Sometimes she begged him to find somebody else, a girl who did not have the wilderness in her soul and a heart of fire. Mary's longing was not for Joseph, but nor was it for any other man. It was a longing that held her poised on the brink of eternity, a longing that beckoned to her from that abyss of anguish and adoration that lies beyond the language of human existence.

That morning, she sat on the edge of the well and slipped off her sandals to feel the warmth of the ground beneath her feet. She raised her skirts and spread her legs to catch the sun on her skin. She lifted her face to the sky and felt the trickle of sweat on her upper lip and on the nape of her neck. Her body felt womanly, ripe, ready for something that belonged not with Joseph but with the wordless desire that beckoned to her from the infinite. So she spread her limbs to the sun and felt the drenching heat of the day on her skin, and there she stayed, eyes shut, singing her desire in the silence of her heart as she had done so often before, a woman clothed in the sun, naked and shameless in the depths of her soul.

Sometimes, passers-by would stare at her when she sat like that, and accuse her of wantonness. People in the village gossipped about her, fearing her strangeness. Mary was like all the other girls in the village, and yet she was not like them. She was too free in her movements, too ecstatic in her joy, too secret in her prayers. She made them uncomfortable, although they could not say why. All this she knew, but it did not tame her or frighten her.

That morning, there were no passers-by, only the road winding to the village, and a ruche of blue hills on the horizon as if God had pressed his knuckles into the earth before the clay was dry, and above and beyond them all the morning sky bleaching to white in the risen light of the sun. Her solitude encompassed the world, and she heard the sound of her longing in the silence, in the birdsong, in the breath of a breeze that came from nowhere and rustled the grass and cooled the sweat on her skin.

And then the breeze was more than the movement of air and the absence of life. The breeze was touch and voice, intimate joy of a lover's caress on her virginal flesh. She yielded, succumbed to the feathery stroke of the light on her skin and the answer at last to her nameless desire. Then gripped by a sudden terror, she opened her eyes and scanned the empty horizon. 'Who are you?' she said. 'How can this be?'

From the horizon came the response, so that she yielded herself to the warm embrace of the day and parted her lips to murmur her delight. 'Yes,' she whispered. 'Let it be.'

I have heard her tell the story so often, but I never grow tired of it. I share Mary's hunger and longing, and I would give my soul to share that eternal moment of ecstacy. No wonder she never wanted a man after that. When a woman discovers such joy in the arms of a man, she is left more hungry and alone than ever before. What Mary discovered that day has never left her. She carries it within her, that secret joy that has proved stronger than all the hardship and pain of her life. What I have found and lost again with many men, Mary has found with no man and never lost.

What is it like to be a woman whose love dared the absolute, a woman who refused to open herself for anyone but God? Mary gained in her own flesh and blood that which Eve has craved in all women for all time, the taste and the knowledge and the likeness of God.

She lifts the cup and sips the wine, and her eyes are dark with the coming night. But in the depths of Mary's soul, there is still I think the glowing ember of that inextinguishable joy.

And then she looks at Joseph over the rim of her glass, and their eyes meet as they share the wine of their affliction and hope. Joseph married her and became father to the child she bore, to save her from scandal and maybe from stoning. Yet Mary's calling was with Jesus, not with Joseph, and after the wedding at Cana she became a disciple, joining us all in our travels and our adventures. Joseph was an old man by then, and wearied by the demands of his life with this woman and her child. He knew that he belonged to something that was passing and that his role was limited. Jesus was making a world without fathers, for we only have one father in heaven. The future belonged to his earthly mother and his heavenly father, not to the gentle man who watched over his childhood years. Quiet and faithful Joseph lives in a small house in Arimathea and he always joins us for the passover, to give thanks for the woman and her child. Yet he is afraid too, afraid of the harm that the Romans might do, afraid still of our own people who have never quite forgotten the scandal of Mary's pregnancy, have never quite forgiven him for his loss of pride and for the indignity he suffered in marrying a woman who was pregnant by another.

REMEMBRANCE

MARTHA

The night wears on and we become mellow with food and wine. There are good-natured arguments, reminiscences, details already forgotten in the telling. Matthew, Mark, and Luke are speaking with the brash confidence of men who have drunk too much. They recall that day when Jesus preached his strange message about the blessings and promises of God for those who hunger and thirst, for those who suffer and mourn. Jesus is quiet, listening and watching but saying little. There's an intensity about the way he listens, as if he is taking in every detail of their conversation.

'I'll never forget it,' says Matthew, leaning back and folding his hands on his belly. 'All those people, and him up on that mountain, with his great voice ringing out. Eh, Lord, you had them all listening that day, I'll tell you that.' Jesus smiles lovingly at this burly disciple with his ruddy face.

'He wasn't up on a mountain,' says Luke. 'We were on the plains that day.' Luke is a refined man. I think he is offended by Matthew's lack of delicacy. He speaks slowly and carefully, as if trying to prevent the wine from blurring the edges of his words.

'No, we might have been on the plains, but the Lord was definitely up a mountain. Weren't you Lord?'

'If you say so,' says Jesus, with a flash of mischief in his smile so that for a moment he looks like a small boy amused at the preoccupations of the adult world.

Matthew belches contentedly. 'I'd like to write a book about that day,' he says. 'I'd call it 'The Sermon on the Mount.''

'But you can't write. None of us can, except Luke,' says Mark.

'I can write,' says Lydia. Lydia comes from Syrophoenicia, and she worship the goddesses of the earth and the harvest. Her daughter and she wear amulets around their necks and wrists and make offerings of grain to their goddesses. Even tonight, as Jesus blessed the cup and the bread, I noticed Lydia and her daughter, Phoebe, sitting beside one another at the end of the table, murmuring their prayers to the goddess and putting aside a piece of bread in her honour.

Lydia is educated, and she has a power of learning in her speech that the rest of us do not have. She is like a teacher to Jesus, explaining to him the writings of the Greek philosophers and the beliefs of the people who worship gods other than Yahweh, the God of Israel. She has studied the works of a philosopher called Plato, and when she speaks of this man to Jesus I see a strange fascination in him. Sometimes he asks her questions that she cannot answer, and then she becomes pensive as if he has opened doors in her mind that were closed before. But at other times she challenges him, and she seems to open doors in his mind too. That's how it was the first time she approached him, and asked him to cast the devil out of her daughter. It was as if Jesus knew that she was somebody who would understand the riddles of his speech, for he told her that he would not take the children's food and throw it to the house-dogs. 'Ah

105

yes, sir,' she replied, quick as a flash, 'but even the house-dogs under the table can eat the children's scraps.' Jesus looked at her in astonishment mingled with respect. I had the sense that she had revealed something to him, something about the nature of his work that he had not realized before. He seemed exhilarated to discover somebody who could match the agility of his speech.

Now Lydia and Phoebe have become disciples. They sit at table with us and eat the same food and listen to the teachings of Jesus, but they still worship their goddesses and make incantations to the moon and the seasons. Sometimes Rachel and Mary of Magdala and my sister join them, and it is beautiful to watch as the five of them sing and dance in the milky fullness of the moon.

Peter complains to Jesus. He says that they are guilty of idolatry, that it is a scandal for the followers of a rabbi to behave in this way. But then Jesus asks Peter who made the moon and the music, who gave life and movement to the women's bodies that they could paint the beauty of their dances on the canvas of the night? How Peter struggles to understand. He loves Jesus so much, but he does not understand him.

The men ignore Lydia when she says that she can write, as if women's skills do not count. I have seen Lydia sometimes at the end of the day, writing a diary in Greek which describes all the teachings and the miracles and the actions of Jesus. If they asked her, she would know whether Jesus preached on a hill or on a plain, and exactly what he said. But Jesus and Lydia exchange glances over the table, conspirators in their silence, letting the men ramble on with their muddled memories.

'What about the day the Lord fed all those people,' says Mark, changing the subject. 'How many do you reckon there were? A thousand?'

'More than that,' says Luke.

'I'd say five thousand. There were five thousand and more,' says Matthew.

'I think the men alone probably numbered about four thousand,' says Luke. 'It would be nearer ten if you counted the women and children.'

'Since when did you ever count us?' says my sister.

She's in a strange mood tonight. I can't fathom what I see on her face. Her cheeks are pale and her eyes are flashing with something I have never seen before. Is it fear, or what? It's not really fair to say that to Luke, because he does notice women and children, at least more than some of the others do. He listens when we speak, and he respects us as disciples and not just as cooks and housekeepers. I see Luke weighing up whether or not to argue with her and then deciding against it.

My sister and John sit on either side of Jesus. John leans against him, his body sculpted with pain. I never know with John whether it is his wounded body or his wounded spirit that aches most when I see his face etched with suffering as it is tonight. Like Jesus, he also seems to be listening attentively to Matthew, Mark, and Luke, as if he shares their recollections but glimpses something else, something perhaps just beyond the horizon of their vision.

There is a secret bond between Luke and John. Do the others sense it too? Sometimes, I wonder if Luke is showing John that men's bodies can express beauty and joy. Do they revisit the circumstances of John's wounding in the quiet night hours, and make it a source of loving instead?

Lazarus sits beside me, on the other side from Judas' empty space. I can feel the living warmth of his upper arm against mine. Lazarus too has a wounded spirit, as if somewhere within himself he carries the chill of the tomb and knows that one day he must return there a second time. But Lazarus hides his pain, and only when we are alone together does he sometimes rest his head on my breast and weep with fear and confusion.

I look sideways at him, enjoying the solid warmth of his presence. His body has recovered from the ordeal of illness and death, and his muscles ripple in his arm as he reaches out for the cup in front of him. Sometimes he is like a tree that I want to shelter beneath. Out of this mutual sheltering and companionship I feel something flowing between us, not the raging whirlpools of passion but a stream of gentleness and trust which might carry us together through life.

The children around the table are beginning to look tired. The older ones are glassy-eyed, and two of the little ones have fallen asleep on their mothers' knees. Little Hannah climbs onto Jesus' knee and falls asleep in his arms. My sister rests her head on his shoulder, and I am transfixed by the beauty of their bodies, Hannah with her soft curls nestling on his breast, Mary with her dark tempestuous beauty draped against his body, John, suffering and broken but resting against him like a child, and Jesus in their midst with his great, quiet love reaching out to us all.

I become conscious of Peter watching them too, his lips curling in disapproval at my sister's behaviour. He suspects that Jesus and she are lovers, but I think that for the first time in her life Mary has discovered a love that is more of the spirit than the body. Yet looking at them in such tender closeness, I find myself wishing they were lovers, hoping that one day they might marry and my sister's soul will find a resting place at last.

HOPE

MARTHA

Outside, a horse clatters past and we hear the bark of a soldier shouting at the people to get out of his way. Then there's a commotion, voices raised in fury and terror. We wait, listening. Peter goes to the window and looks out. Andrew joins him, and James. I see Ruth instinctively cupping her hands around her belly, as if to cover the ears of the child in her womb.

'What's happening?' asks Rachel.

'They're throwing stones at the soldier. He has drawn his sword,' says Peter. We hear the sound of more horses, more voices. I squeeze in between Peter and Andrew and look out in time to see the flash of a sword in the moonlight and a scuffle as the soldier strikes a man. There's a howl, and then silence as shock seizes the crowd. The soldier quickly mounts his horse and rides away with the others, so that it's over as suddenly as it started. The sound of their horses fades away over the cobbled streets, and then we hear the wailing of the women who gather around the bleeding body of the man they killed.

'What are we doing, cowering in here like frightened women?' Peter is shouting. He has turned away from the window and he strides across the room to confront Jesus. 'You've turned us into women, all of us. Weak, pathetic, snivelling women!' Jesus says nothing. Peter is quivering with rage. He turns to face the other disciples. 'If we are real men, we'll take our swords now and go out and fight for our people.'

The men look from Jesus to Peter, waiting for guidance. They've forgotten what it is to be men who strut into the streets and fight. Jesus wipes his hands over his face. The graze on his cheek has formed a bloodied crust, and his eye is swollen and bruised. He stands up, and then slowly he goes into the hallway where the men have left their swords. He comes back carrying Peter's sword. He goes to stand in front of Peter, extending the sword between his hands.

'Here is your sword, Peter. Go and fight if you want to. I won't be with you forever. You must decide how you will live when I'm gone. But remember, if you live by the sword, you will also die by the sword.' Peter hesitates, then he reaches out and takes the sword from Jesus.

'What else are we to live by, in a world such as this?' he says, and there's menace in his voice and in the stroke of his hand on the hilt of the sword.

And then, while Jesus faces Peter in silence, we hear the sound of singing from the street below. We go to the window and huddle together, trying to see what's happening. The crowd has dispersed, and the street is empty except for the body of the man who was killed, and a woman who kneels beside him. She has cradled his head on her lap, and she is singing a lament to the night. His blood glistens darkly on the pavement, reflecting the glint of her hair in the moonlight. Her voice is liquid with grief and with love. She strokes his hair and she sings as if by her lullaby she might sing him gently into another world.

'There is a better way, Peter. There is a better way.' Jesus' voice is barely a whisper, so that he is speaking more to himself than to Peter. He goes to the harp that stands in a corner of the room, ready for the time after the meal when we will sing and dance together while he plays music, as we always do when we celebrate the passover together. He carries the harp to the window, and there, framed against the rooftops and the night and bathed in moonlight, he begins to accompany the woman's sad lament. Standing beside him, I see the woman lift her face, but she doesn't interrupt her song. She half-smiles, acknowledging him, and their music slips through the boundaries of time and space and catches us up in some eternal moment, lingering over the city as if it has become the voice of all the suffering of the past and the future. And then there is a movement in the room, and my sister begins to dance.

She is not my sister, but a flame that the music kindles into life. She moves with the stroke of his hand and the words of the song. She gives shape to the woman's grief, and human form to the ancient music of the harp. They are in perfect harmony, one with the other. Every ripple of her limbs, every note of the music, every word of the song, evoke one another, calling, responding, each bringing the other into being at every moment so that they exist only for and with each other. They are not three but one, the voice that sings in the street, the music that flows from his fingertips, the patterns of movement and light that my sister traces in the air. His mother Mary begins to sing, and then the rest of us join in. My sister reaches out and takes my hand, so that my body moves with hers and learns from her, until I too have become part of the song and the music and the dance. So it spreads among us, until we become one body, one life, one spirit in him, in his music and in the power of his love.

MARY

This body is mine, but not mine. It has become the music he plays, the song that she sings. I have not left my body, rather my body has found me, has taken on the liquid contours of my soul so that now it flows and sculpts itself into the air, and it knows, I know, for the very first time. The marriage bed, the grave, the womb, the tomb, these are not the spheres that separate life and death, joy and terror, for all are held together in the music he plays. In death we are in life, in our mourning there is joy, in the lament of the woman drifting up from the street there is hope, for only a woman who hopes would dare to sing a lullaby to a corpse.

His mother comes to him, and she takes up the song of the woman in the street, and in her voice I hear again the voice of Eve who sang in a garden and loved too much and whose desire was too brave and too reckless for the world of men. And I know, I know as I listen to the song of his mother, that Eve was not wrong, it's just that our world was not ready for her. Perhaps the world is not ready yet. But the hour has come. The hour when we must become what we are not yet. Like the unseen woman who sings in the street we must dare to cradle the past in our arms, and sing of our hope to the stars.

Does Mary look at this man in our midst, and see in him the fulfilment of her hunger for God? I watch them, the way she kneels beside him, the sense of the oneness that holds them together, and I think that beyond every longing of the mortal flesh, he is the desire of Mary's heart.

And of mine. How I desire him. But I have desired men before for the passionate thrill of their touch and their breath that whispers their love, and although I want him like that too, that is not the shape of my longing, not the fulfilment of my dreams. Other men cannot touch what he touches in me, and yet he has never touched me as other men do. But now, his music is more than touch, more than desire, more than joy, more than words.

So here I dissolve, and I dance, and I close my eyes, and I do not leave my body but inhabit it for the very first time. I forget everything else, the other bodies dancing beside me, the remains of the meal on the table, the city beyond the window. I feel the pulse in my neck, throbbing against my skin. I see the red glow of my eyelids against the light. I feel the push of my breasts against my dress, the stroke of my skirt against my thighs, the caress of my naked feet on the floor. Eyes closed, head back, hair trailing against the burnish of lamplight, I quiver with the life that speaks beyond words. I part my lips to feel the honeyed air on my tongue, and I breathe its sweetness into my lungs. My arms lift, weightless, above my head, and I begin to spin. Slowly at first, then more quickly, my feet a drumbeat that matches my pulse to the music, my body swirling, my skirt a billowing halo of joy.

Then the music has gone, ripped away from the fabric of night by a gesture too violent to bear. I open my eyes. Peter stands in front of Jesus, and he has grabbed hold of his harp.

'This is obscene. You mock us with your filth.' Although he was facing Jesus at the start, by the time he says the word 'filth' he is glaring at me.

116

I feel my dancing wither on my limbs in the face of his scorn. The woman's voice in the street tapers into silence, and we all gaze at one another, suddenly helpless in the face of so much discord and anger, so many broken dreams and blighted visions. We hear the voices of others muttering in the streets, men who have come to take the body away, polluting themselves with the taint of death on this holy night of our deliverance. Afterwards they will wash, enacting the rituals that seduce us into believing we can indeed escape the all-pervasive taint and purify ourselves from the stench of the corpse that rots neglected in the violent night.

I sit down, and the others too flop around the room, breathless with the dancing, heavy with the eating and drinking, weary with the fear that grips us all. But Jesus starts strumming his harp again, although I see that his spirit too is exhausted and longs for rest. His mother watches him, and in her stillness I know the dance continues in her soul. Her sorrow tonight is boundless, but it is the sorrow of an infinite faith, an infinite trust in the goodness of God. She goes to her dark-eyed son strumming his harp, and she rests her hand on his head. I think of Sarah and Abraham, and of the promise made to our people. I think of my sister's declaration, 'You are the Messiah,' and now I do not allow my mind to run away from the thought. I remember the anointing, the fragrance of the oil, the passion of my soul, the language of death and burial, and I recall that there is another anointing, the anointing of kingship.

I look at him and I know that I have anointed a king, then I wonder why I should think such a thing. He is after all just a peasant like the rest of us, his mother is a poor village woman. But in this golden moment they are Solomon and the Queen of Sheba, jewelled in candlelight and luminous with the spirit of the dance and the music that plays on their souls.

She begins to sing now, and her voice is rich and deep. She sings Hannah's song, the ancient hymn of our people that she sang when she visited Elizabeth in the early days of her pregnancy. 'My soul magnifies the Lord, and my spirit rejoices in God my Saviour.' He closes his eyes and hums to himself as she sings, as if reminding himself of something that he has forgotten, some memory that eludes him. Then Elizabeth comes to stand beside them, and her voice is like the rustle of dry leaves in a winter wind. Elizabeth, Mary and Jesus, with the spirit of Elizabeth's dead son hovering in their midst, like one crying in the wilderness, 'Behold, the lamb of God.'

NIGHT

MARY

The men have fallen asleep, and the air is thick with their belches and farts and snores. They have eaten and drunk too well, and they are terrified. They sense the dread in the air, but they are afraid to read the signs. They cannot bear the torment of wakefulness, the consciousness of his pain. He has always comforted and consoled them, but now, when his need is so great, they have nothing to give.

So often, he has craved solitude and tried to escape the ever-present crowds. I have seen him sometimes, drained and exhausted, longing for a few moments of silence but always the people kept coming, with their suffering bodies and wounded spirits and longing for wholeness and joy. But tonight, for the first time, it seems he cannot bear his own company. He has been forsaken by that inner peace, that sense of being at one with himself, which has so often spread itself like an aura over the rest of us. What did Judas take from him when he fled into the night?

And now only the women keep watch and pray, huddled together for warmth. His mother is there, and Mary Salome, and Martha, and Mary wife of Clopas. Mary of Magdala sits a little apart from them, staring in silence at the moon, her eyes wide with fear. I wonder if she hears the whispers of her abandoned demons taunting her, seducing her back into madness. Perhaps it would be better to laugh wild and naked at the moon, than to gaze at it through the eyes of cold and frightened sanity.

I suddenly need to be alone. I creep away from them, picking my way by moonlight among the stones and shrubs to the gates of a nearby garden, putting a distance between us. I slip through the gates in search of solitude, and then I see him, and he too is alone.

I stand beneath a gnarled old fruit tree, watching him. I lean on the tree and try to draw strength from the sap that rises deep within its scarred and knotted trunk. The wood beneath my hand speaks of a hidden energy that flows from generation to generation, reminding me that there are forms of life more ancient and more enduring than the shadows and dreams that mark the space of our human existence.

He kneels with his elbows on a rock and his face turned to the sky. His body looks grey in the moonlight. I have seen him take on the hues and the contours of the wilderness. Standing in the midday sun, I have gazed at the bronze hills that are sculpted out of the land, and I have seen the shape of his body, vast, one with the earth, stretched out and giving form and meaning to all that is. But now he is carved out of stone, and his body has absorbed the chilled, forsaken spirit of the night.

I am close enough to see him trembling, and the moon makes dark crystals of his tears. The graze on his cheek is bleeding, so that his tears leave streaks of blood on his face. I have seen his emotions before, this man who feels with such intensity and passion, but I have never seen him like this. His fear crosses the small space between us, and I feel my knees weaken, my own limbs begin to quiver. I force myself to stand still. I am afraid to breathe. I am so still that a small snake slithers across my sandal, and I feel its dry touch on my toes like the caress of a friend. That is how my hair must have felt on his feet that night, when I anointed him.

His breath snags in the air, ragged and dry. He groans, and his voice makes the ground tilt beneath my feet. God. Where are you?

For three years he has preached God's love to the poor, the outcast, the broken-hearted. Three years of promising forgiveness to sinners, comfort to those who mourn, food to the hungry, release to the captives. Three years of exhaustion and exhilaration. Three years of giving himself day after day, month after month, to the people who never stop coming. Three years of showing us the face of a God who cares despite all the evidence we have to the contrary. And now, where is his caring God? A man's body, small and vulnerable in the enormity of night, has become the focus of all the broken-hearted, all the hungry, all the mourners and prisoners of history. Look God, if you would offer a father's love, your son is crying for you. Have you no pity?

Who is this God who treats the one he loves with such contempt? Where is this loving father, when his son is crying? God is not here. He has forsaken his beloved one.

What was the point of it all? Why should he not have lived as any other man? He would have been such a wonderful lover, such a perfect father. And why do I speak in the past tense, as if such things cannot be? Why should he not still be a lover and father?

His God is as cold and dead as the rock he leans on. But I am here. If God will not comfort his tormented soul, why should I not go to him instead?

I am warm and alive. My body hungers for his. I will hold his head against my breast and my fingers will write the words of my loving on his flesh. I will show him the comfort of a woman's love, until he forgets his cruel, unseeing God.

He is a man who knows women more intimately and more lovingly than any man I have ever known, but he has never claimed for himself the joy of a woman's body. The love I feel for him has yearned to speak the language of the body as well as the spirit and the heart. What harm could it do, for him to come to my bed as once Lazarus came to my bed to find solace in the secret hours of the night?

Lazarus. A man of such vigour and beauty and tenderness, until the fever took hold of him. Martha and I did all that we could to nurse him, but hour by hour his life was slipping away. We sent for Jesus, knowing that only a miracle would save Lazarus. Then there were the long hours of waiting, his life dissolving in the vapour of his breath and the heat of his flesh. There was the slow realization that Jesus was not going to come. When we needed him most, he had let us down. That was almost as hard to bear as the death of Lazarus.

He died in my arms, and I held the body that had given me such delight until his limbs stiffened and the coldness of death laid its hands upon him. Then I lay on the bed and mourned for three days, until they told me that Jesus had arrived, and my fury drove me out onto the streets to confront him.

When Lazarus stepped from the tomb, his body was one that had known the intimate caress of death even although his limbs were supple again and his skin had lost the pallor of the grave. In that moment, I began to know something that tonight I know more clearly still, but I do not know what it is.

I watched them, side by side, Jesus and Lazarus, and it was as if both had been kissed by the angel of death. Yet the kiss of death remained on Lazarus' brow, even as he stood in the sunlight looking as he had always looked. I knew that one day Lazarus would die again, and another woman would hold his body and weep, but it would not be me. Something in me had died with Lazarus, and that which came to life again when Lazarus stepped from the tomb was altogether new. Unlike Lazarus, I was not the person I had been.

And Jesus? The encounter with death had achieved some strange transfiguration in him. For a moment, he shed the mortal confines of his body. I saw some force of life that I did not know existed, some life that must not always declare its presence against the all-consuming tide of death. That same life was kindled in me when I heard him calling to Lazarus to come out from the tomb. From that moment, I knew that I would love Jesus and no other man.

Now I see Lazarus and Martha gazing at each other, and there is about them that aura of two who are falling in love. They will not know the frenzied pleasure of bodies that Lazarus knew with me, and Martha will not take his spirit to the horizon as I did. But I think they will be married soon, and widows and children and the lonely strangers of the city will find warmth and comfort in their home, and the raising of Lazarus will not have been in vain.

I did love him, and I miss his caresses. But even Lazarus, who loved me so passionately, had moments of forgetfulness when I was not Mary, the woman he knew, but a body he claimed in darkness. His eyes would skim the surface of my face, so that he penetrated my body but not my soul. He was heavy on top of me, seeking his own pleasure, his body clamouring for satisfaction. Then his loving became a form of possession, and afterwards I would lie beside him as a stranger and long for the morning when he would be Lazarus again, familiar and gentle and loving.

Would Jesus be like that? Never have I known his love to lay claim to another's body or soul, or to express itself with force. He offers himself with such freedom and joy, and asks nothing in exchange. But maybe for women there is always some transaction involved, some debt repaid for the gift of love, when men take possession of our bodies.

But to go to him freely, to give myself as he gives, abundantly, asking nothing in return, to give him that knowledge which he does not possess, the knowledge of a woman's body and the kindling of my desire, there would be no harm in that. And if the terror of this night continues to unfold, if some unforeseen calamity lies in wait just around the corner of daybreak, at least he might remember and draw comfort from the lingering touch of my flesh on his.

There might be a child, a child who would have the shape of his mouth and the curve of his cheek and the glow of his eyes. Whatever awaits him, I could teach his child to be like him, to continue his work, to preach his message. Yes, even if in the end his God forsakes him, I will teach his child about the fatherly love of God and hold out the promise of love and forgiveness to a world made callous by an excess of pain.

I step back more deeply into the shadows. Carefully, I wriggle out of my clothes, letting them fall in a pile at my feet. Moonbeams trickle through the leaves and dance on my skin. My breasts are fruits that ripen sweetly for the picking. My body was made for this moment. He and I, we were both made for this.

I look at him again. He has cradled his head in his hands. What is he thinking? What is he praying for? His loneliness overwhelms me. This man, who has never been granted the solitude he craves, is utterly alone now when he has pleaded with his friends not to leave him.

I step forward out of the shadows. A light breeze whispers between us, bringing with it the smell of jasmine and orange blossom, but also the smell of his sweat and his fear, mingled with the smell of the bread and the wine that we shared. But the breeze brings more than fragrance and memory. I hear a distant clamour of voices, as if an angry crowd is gathering over towards the city. My flesh prickles, and I retreat back into the shade. Jesus lifts his head, poised and listening to that faraway clamour on the edges of darkness. I know that there is little time. I must go to him quickly, or it will be too late.

I pick up my linen shift from the ground and slide it over my nakedness. I go quietly to his side. He says my name, but that is all. We have no need for words.

I kneel beside him and I take his cold hands between mine. The voices are getting louder, and now I see the flames of their torches sparking in the distance among the trees. We kneel in silence for a long time, and then he says,

'Don't leave me.'

'I will never leave you.'

I stay with him until their torches appear at the gates of the garden like angels bearing swords of fire.

Then Judas gives him the kiss I did not dare.